ON A
HAPPY LIFE

Lucius Annæus
Seneca

First published 2020
Copyright © 2020 Aziloth Books

All Rights Reserved. No part of this publication may be reproduced, stored in a retrieval system or transmitted in any form or by any means, electronic, mechanical, photocopying, recording, scanning or otherwise, except under the terms of the Copyright Licensing Agency Ltd, 90 Tottenham Court Road, London, W1P 0LP, UK, without the permission in writing of the Publisher. Requests to the Publisher should be via email to: info@azilothbooks.com.

Every effort has been made to contact all copyright holders. The publisher will be glad to make good in future editions any errors or omissions brought to their attention.

This publication is designed to provide authoritative and accurate information in regard to the subject matter covered. It is sold on the understanding that the Publisher is not engaged in rendering professional services.

British Library Cataloguing in Publication Data

A catalogue record for this book is available from the British Library

ISBN-13: 978-1-913751-04-3

Cover Illustration:

Nero and Seneca (plaster, partially polychromed)
Eduardo Barron (1904). Museo del Prado.

CONTENTS

CHAPTER I	OF A HAPPY LIFE, AND WHEREIN IT CONSISTS	6
CHAPTER II	HUMAN HAPPINESS IS FOUNDED UPON WISDOM AND VIRTUE; AND FIRST, OF WISDOM	8
CHAPTER III	THERE CAN BE NO HAPPINESS WITHOUT VIRTUE	11
CHAPTER IV	PHILOSOPHY IS THE GUIDE OF LIFE	16
CHAPTER V	THE FORCE OF PRECEPTS	22
CHAPTER VI	NO FELICITY LIKE PEACE OF CONSCIENCE	26
CHAPTER VII	A GOOD MAN CAN NEVER BE MISERABLE, NOR A WICKED MAN HAPPY	29
CHAPTER VIII	THE DUE CONTEMPLATION OF DIVINE PROVIDENCE IS THE CERTAIN CURE OF ALL MISFORTUNES	32
CHAPTER IX	OF LEVITY OF MIND, AND OTHER IMPEDIMENTS OF A HAPPY LIFE	37
CHAPTER X	HE THAT SETS UP HIS REST UPON CONTINGENCIES SHALL NEVER BE QUIET	41
CHAPTER XI	A SENSUAL LIFE IS A MISERABLE LIFE	45
CHAPTER XII	AVARICE AND AMBITION ARE INSATIABLE & RESTLESS	49
CHAPTER XIII	HOPE AND FEAR ARE THE BANE OF HUMAN LIFE	53
CHAPTER XIV	IT IS ACCORDING TO THE TRUE OR FALSE ESTIMATE OF THINGS THAT WE ARE HAPPY OR MISERABLE	56
CHAPTER XV	THE BLESSINGS OF TEMPERANCE & MODERATION	58
CHAPTER XVI	CONSTANCY OF MIND GIVES A MAN REPUTATION, & MAKES HIM HAPPY IN DESPITE OF ALL MISFORTUNE	63
CHAPTER XVII	OUR HAPPINESS DEPENDS IN A GREAT MEASURE UPON THE CHOICE OF OUR COMPANY	69
CHAPTER XVIII	THE BLESSINGS OF FRIENDSHIP	72
CHAPTER XIX	HE THAT WOULD BE HAPPY MUST TAKE AN ACCOUNT OF HIS TIME	75

CHAPTER XX	HAPPY IS THE MAN THAT MAY CHOOSE HIS OWN BUSINESS	79
CHAPTER XXI	THE CONTEMPT OF DEATH MAKES ALL THE MISERIES OF LIFE EASY TO US	83
CHAPTER XXII	CONSOLATIONS AGAINST DEATH, FROM THE PROVIDENCE & THE NECESSITY OF IT	89
CHAPTER XXIII	AGAINST IMMODERATE SORROW FOR THE DEATH OF FRIENDS	92
CHAPTER XXIV	CONSOLATION AGAINST BANISHMENT AND BODILY PAIN.	96
CHAPTER XXV	POVERTY TO A WISE MAN IS RATHER A BLESSING THAN A MISFORTUNE	98

ADDENDUM: SENECA'S LIFE - AND DEATH   102

On a Happy Life

translated by Sir Robert L'Estrange

.CHAPTER I.
ON A HAPPY LIFE, AND WHEREIN IT CONSISTS.

There is not any thing in this world, perhaps, that is more talked of, and less understood, than the business of *a happy life*. It is every man's wish and design; and yet not one of a thousand that knows wherein that happiness consists. We live, however, in a blind and eager pursuit of it; and the more haste we make in a wrong way, the further we are from our journey's end. Let us therefore, *first*, consider "what it is we should be at"; and, *secondly*, "which is the readiest way to compass it." If we be right, we shall find every day how much we improve; but if we either follow the cry, or the track, of people that are out of the way, we must expect to be misled, and to continue our days in wandering in error. Wherefore, it highly concerns us to take along with us a skilful guide; for it is not in this, as in other voyages, where the highway brings us to our place of repose; or if a man should happen to be out, where the inhabitants might set him right again: but on the contrary, the beaten road is here the most dangerous, and the people, instead of helping us, misguide us.

Let us not therefore follow, like beasts, but rather govern ourselves by *reason*, than by *example*. It fares with us in human life as in a routed army; one stumbles first, and then another falls upon him, and so they follow, one upon the neck of another, until the whole field comes to be but one heap of miscarriages. And the mischief is, "that the number of the multitude carries it against truth and justice;" so that we must leave the crowd, if we would be happy: for the question of a *happy life* is not to be decided by vote: nay, so far from it, that plurality of voices is an argument of the wrong; the common people find it easier to believe than to judge, and content themselves with what is usual, never examining whether it be good or not. By *the common people* is intended the *man of title* as well as the *clouted shoe*: for I do not distinguish them by the eye, but by the mind, which is the proper judge of the man. Worldly felicity, I know, makes the head giddy; but if ever a man comes to himself again, he will confess, that "whatsoever he has done, he wishes undone;" and that "the things he feared were better than those he prayed for."

The true felicity of life is to be free from perturbations, to understand our duties towards God and man: to enjoy the present without any anxious dependence upon the future. Not to amuse ourselves with either hopes or fears, but to rest satisfied with what we have, which is abundantly sufficient; for he that is so, wants nothing. The great blessings of mankind are within us, and within our reach; but we shut our eyes, and, like people in the dark, we fall foul upon the very thing which we search for without finding it. "Tranquillity is a certain equality of mind, which no condition of fortune can either exalt or depress." Nothing can make it less: for it is the state of human perfection: it raises us as high as we can go; and makes every man his own supporter; whereas he that is borne up by any thing else may fall. He that judges aright, and perseveres in it, enjoys a perpetual calm: he takes a true prospect of things; he observes an order, measure, a decorum in all his actions; he has a benevolence in his nature; he squares his life according to reason; and draws to himself love and admiration. Without a certain and an unchangeable judgment, all the rest is but fluctuation: but "he that always wills and nills the same thing, is undoubtedly in the right."

Liberty and serenity of mind must necessarily ensue upon the mastering of those things which either allure or affright us; when instead of those flashy pleasures, (which even at the best are both vain and hurtful together,) we shall find ourselves possessed of joy transporting and everlasting. It must be a *sound mind* that makes a *happy man*; there must be a constancy in all conditions, a care for the things of this world, but without trouble; and such an indifferency for the bounties of fortune, that either with them, or without them, we may live contentedly. There must be neither lamentation, nor quarrelling, nor sloth, nor fear; for it makes a discord in a man's life. "He that fears, serves."

The joy of a wise man stands firm without interruption; in all places, at all times, and in all conditions, his thoughts are cheerful and quiet. As it never *came in* to him from *without*, so it will never leave him; but it is born within him, and inseparable from him. It is a solicitous life that is egged on with the hope of any thing, though never so open and easy, nay, though a man should never suffer any sort of disappointment. I do not speak this either as a bar to the fair enjoyment of lawful pleasures, or to the gentle flatteries of reasonable expectations: but, on the contrary, I would have men to be always in good humor, provided that it arises from their own souls, and be cherished in their own breasts. Other delights are trivial; they may smooth the brow, but they do not fill and affect the heart. "True joy is a serene and sober motion;" and they are miserably out that take *laughing* for *rejoicing*. The seat of it is within, and there is no cheerfulness like the resolution of a brave mind, that has fortune under his feet. He that can look death in the face, and bid it welcome; open his door to poverty, and bridle his appetites; this is the man whom Providence has established in the possession of inviolable delights. The pleasures of the vulgar are ungrounded, thin, and superficial; but the others are solid and *eternal*.

As the *body* itself is rather a *necessary thing*, than a *great*; so the comforts of it are but temporary and vain; beside that, without extraordinary moderation, their end is only pain and repentance; whereas a peaceful conscience, honest thoughts, virtuous actions, and an indifference for casual events, are blessings without end, satiety, or measure. This consummated state of felicity is only a submission to the dictate of right nature; "The foundation of it is wisdom and virtue; the knowledge of what we ought to do, and the conformity of the will to that knowledge."

CHAPTER II.
HUMAN HAPPINESS IS FOUNDED UPON WISDOM AND VIRTUE; AND FIRST, OF WISDOM.

Taking for granted that *human happiness* is founded upon *wisdom* and *virtue* we shall treat of these two points in order as they lie: and, *first*, of *wisdom*; not in the latitude of its various operations but as it has only a regard to good life, and the happiness of mankind.

Wisdom is a right understanding, a faculty of discerning good from evil; what is to be chosen, and what rejected; a judgment grounded upon the value of things, and not the common opinion of them; an equality of force, and a strength of resolution.

It sets a watch over our words and deeds, it takes us up with the contemplation of the works of nature, and makes us invincible by either good or evil fortune. It is large and spacious, and requires a great deal of room to work in; it ransacks heaven and earth; it has for its object things past and to come, transitory and eternal. It examines all the circumstances of time; "what it is, when it began, and how long it will continue: and so for the mind; whence it came; what it is; when it begins; how long it lasts; whether or not it passes from one form to another, or serves only one and wanders when it leaves us; whether it abides in a state of separation, and what the action of it; what use it makes of its liberty; whether or not it retains the memory of things past, and comes to the knowledge of itself."

It is the habit of a perfect mind, and the perfection of humanity, raised as high as Nature can carry it. It differs from *philosophy*, as avarice and money; the one desires, and the other is desired; the one is the effect and the reward of the other. To be wise is the use of wisdom, as seeing is the use of eyes, and well-speaking the use of eloquence. He that is perfectly wise is perfectly happy; nay, the very beginning of wisdom makes life easy to us. Neither is it enough to know this, unless we print it in our minds by daily meditation, and so bring a *good-will* to a good habit. And we must practice what we preach: for *philosophy* is not a subject for popular ostentation; nor does it rest in words, but in things. It is not an entertainment taken up for delight, or to give a taste to our leisure; but it fashions the mind, governs our actions, tells us what we are to do, and what not. It sits at the helm, and guides us through all hazards; nay, we cannot be safe without it, for every hour gives us occasion to make use of it. It informs us in all duties of life, piety to our parents, faith to our friends, charity to the miserable, judgment in counsel; it gives us *peace* by *fearing* nothing, and *riches* by *coveting nothing*.

There is no condition of life that excludes a wise man from discharging his duty. If his fortune be good, he *tempers* it; if bad, he *masters* it; if he has an estate, he will exercise his virtue in plenty; if none, in poverty: if he cannot do it in his country, he will do it in banishment; if he has no command, he will do the office of a common soldier.

Some people have the skill of reclaiming the fiercest of beasts; they will make a lion embrace his keeper, a tiger kiss him, and an elephant kneel to him. This is the case of a wise man in the extremest difficulties; let them be never so terrible in themselves, when they come to him once, they are perfectly tame. They that ascribe the invention of tillage, architecture, navigation, etc., to wise men, may perchance be in the right, that they were invented by wise men, as wise men; for wisdom does not teach our fingers, but our minds: fiddling and dancing, arms and fortifications, were the works of luxury and discord; but wisdom instructs us in the way of nature, and in the arts of unity and concord, not in the instruments, but in the government of life; not to make us live only, but to live happily. She teaches us what things are good, what evil, and what only appear so; and to distinguish betwixt true greatness and tumor. She clears our minds of dross and vanity; she raises up our thoughts to heaven, and carries them down to hell: she discourses of the nature of the soul, the powers and faculties of it; the first principles of things; the order of Providence: she exalts us from things corporeal to things incorporeal, and retrieves the truth of all: she searches nature, gives laws to life; and tells us, "That it is not enough to God, unless we obey him": she looks upon all accidents as acts of Providence: sets a true value upon things; delivers us from false opinions, and condemns all pleasures that are attended with repentance. She allows nothing to be good that will not be so forever; no man to be happy but that needs no other happiness than what he has within himself. This is the felicity of human life; a felicity that can neither be corrupted nor extinguished: it inquires into the nature of the heavens, the influence of the stars; how far they operate upon our minds and bodies: which thoughts, though they do not form our manners, they do yet raise and dispose us for glorious things.

It is agreed upon all hands that "right reason is the perfection of human nature," and wisdom only the dictate of it. The greatness that arises from it is solid and unmovable, the resolutions of wisdom being free, absolute and constant; whereas folly is never long pleased with the same thing, but still shifting of counsels and sick of itself. There can be no happiness without constancy and prudence, for a wise man is to write without a blot, and what he likes once he approves for ever. He admits of nothing that is either evil or slippery, but marches without staggering or stumbling, and is never surprised; he lives always true and steady to himself, and whatsoever befalls him, this great artificer of both fortunes turns to advantage; he that demurs and hesitates is not yet composed; but wheresoever virtue interposes upon the main, there must be concord and consent in the parts; for all virtues are in agreement, as well as all vices are at variance. A wise man, in what condition soever he is, will be still happy, for he subjects all things to himself, because he submits himself to reason, and governs his actions by council, not by passion.

He is not moved with the utmost violence of fortune, nor with the extremities of fire and sword; whereas a fool is afraid of his own shadow, and surprised at ill accidents, as if they were all levelled at him. He does nothing unwillingly, for whatever he finds necessary, he makes it his choice. He propounds to himself the certain scope and end of human life: he follows that which conduces to it, and avoids that which hinders it. He is content with his lot whatever it be, without wishing what he has not, though, of the two, he had rather abound than want. The great business of his life, like that of nature, is performed without tumult or noise. He neither fears danger or provokes it, but it is his caution, not any want of courage – for captivity, wounds and chains, he only looks upon as false and lymphatic terrors. He does not pretend to go through with whatever he undertakes, but to do that well which he does. Arts are but the servants – wisdom commands – and where the matter fails it is none of the workman's fault. He is cautelous[1] in doubtful cases, in prosperity temperate, and resolute in adversity, still making the best of every condition and improving all occasions to make them serviceable to his fate. Some accidents there are, which I confess may affect him, but not overthrow him, as bodily pains, loss of children and friends, the ruin and desolation of a man's country. One must be made of stone or iron, not to be sensible of these calamities; and, beside, it were no virtue to bear them, if a body did not feel them.

There are *three degrees of proficients* in the school of wisdom. The *first* are those that come within sight of it, but not up to it – they have learned what they ought to do, but they have not put their knowledge in practice – they are past the hazard of a relapse, but they have still the grudges of a disease, though they are out of the danger of it. By a disease I do understand an obstinacy in evil, or an ill habit, that makes us over-eager upon things which are either not much to be desired, or not at all. A *second* sort are those that have subjected their appetites for a season, but are yet in fear of falling back. A *third* sort are those that are clear of many vices but not of all. They are not covetous, but perhaps they are choleric – nor lustful, but perchance ambitious; they are firm enough in some cases but weak enough in others: there are many that despise death and yet shrink at pain. There are diversities in wise men, but no inequalities – one is more affable, another more ready, a third a better speaker; but the felicity of them all is equal. It is in this as in heavenly bodies, there is a *certain state* in greatness.

In civil and domestic affairs, a wise man may stand in need of counsel, as of a physician, an advocate, a solicitor; but in greater matters, the blessing of wise men rests in the joy they take in the communication of their virtues. If there were nothing else in it, a man would apply himself to wisdom, because it settles him in a perfect tranquillity of mind.

---

1. *cautious; wary; provident*

CHAPTER III.
THERE CAN BE NO HAPPINESS WITHOUT VIRTUE.

Virtue is that perfect good which is the complement of a *happy life*; the only immortal thing that belongs to mortality – it is the knowledge both of others and itself – it is an invincible greatness of mind, not to be elevated or dejected with good or ill fortune. It is sociable and gentle, free, steady, and fearless, content within itself, full of inexhaustible delights, and it is valued for itself. One may be a good physician, a good governor, a good grammarian, without being a good man, so that all things from without are only accessories, for the seat of it is a pure and holy mind. It consists in a congruity of actions which we can never expect so long as we are distracted by our passions: not but that a man may be allowed to change color and countenance, and suffer such impressions as are properly a kind of natural force upon the body, and not under the dominion of the mind; but all this while I will have his judgment firm, and he shall act steadily and boldly, without wavering betwixt the motions of his body and those of his mind.

It is not a thing indifferent, I know, whether a man lies at ease upon a bed, or in torment upon a wheel – and yet the former may be the worse of the two if he suffer the latter with honor, and enjoy the other with infamy. It is not the *matter*, but the *virtue*, that makes the action *good or ill*; and he that is led in triumph may be yet greater than his conqueror.

When we come once to value our flesh above our honesty we are lost: and yet I would not press upon dangers, no, not so much as upon inconveniences, unless where the man and the brute come in competition; and in such a case, rather than make a forfeiture of my credit, my reason, or my faith, I would run all extremities.

They are great blessings to have tender parents, dutiful children, and to live under a just and well-ordered government. Now, would it not trouble even a virtuous man to see his children butchered before his eyes, his father made a slave, and his country overrun by a barbarous enemy? There is a great difference betwixt the simple loss of a blessing and the succeeding of a great mischief in the place of it, over and above. The loss of health is followed with sickness, and the loss of sight with blindness; but this does not hold in the loss of friends and children, where there is rather something to the contrary to supply that loss: that is to say, *virtue*, which fills the mind, and takes away the desire of what we have not. What matters it whether the water be stopped or not, so long as the fountain is safe? Is a man ever the wiser for a multitude of friends, or the more foolish for the loss of them? so neither is he the happier, nor the more miserable. Short life, grief and pain are accessions that have no effect at all upon virtue. It consists in the action and not in the things we do – in the choice itself, and not in the subject-matter of it. It is not a despicable body or condition, nor poverty, infamy or scandal, that can obscure the glories of virtue; but a man may see her through all oppositions: and he that looks diligently into the state of a wicked man will see the canker at his heart, through all the false and dazzling splendors of greatness and fortune. We shall then discover our *childishness*, in setting our hearts upon things trivial and contemptible, and in the selling of our very country and parents for a *rattle*. And what is the difference (in effect) betwixt *old men* and *children*, but that the *one* deals in *paintings* and *statues*, and the *other* in *babies*, so that we ourselves are only the more expensive fools.

If one could but see the mind of a good man, as it is illustrated with virtue; the beauty and the majesty of it, which is a dignity not so much as to be thought of without love and veneration – would not a man bless himself at the sight of such an object as at the encounter of some supernatural power – a power so miraculous that it is a kind of charm upon the souls of those that are truly affected with it. There is so wonderful a grace and authority in it that even the worst of men approve it, and set up for the reputation of being accounted virtuous themselves. They covet the fruit indeed, and the profit of wickedness; but they hate and are ashamed of the imputation of it. It is by an impression of Nature that all men have a reverence for virtue – they know it and they have a respect for it though they do not practice it – nay, for the countenance of their very *wickedness*, they miscall it *virtue*. Their injuries they call *benefits*, and expect a man should thank them for doing him a mischief – they cover their most notorious iniquities with a pretext of justice.

He that robs upon the highway had rather find his booty than force it; ask any of them that live upon rapine, fraud, oppression, if they had not rather enjoy a fortune honestly gotten, and their consciences will not suffer them to deny it. Men are vicious only for the proof of villainy; for at the same time that they commit it they condemn it; nay, so powerful is virtue, and so gracious is Providence, that every man has a light set up within him for a guide, which we do, all of us, both see and acknowledge, though we do not pursue it. This it is that makes the prisoner upon the torture happier than the executioner, and sickness better than health, if we bear it without yielding or repining – this it is that overcomes ill-fortune and moderates good – for it marches betwixt the one and the other, with an equal contempt for both. It turns (like fire) all things into itself, our actions and our friendships are tinctured with it, and whatever it touches becomes amiable.

That which is frail and mortal rises and falls, grows, wastes, and varies from itself; but the state of things divine is always the same; and so is virtue, let the matter be what it will. It is never the worse for the difficulty of the action, nor the better for the easiness of it. It is the same in a rich man as in a poor; in a sickly man as in a sound; in a strong as in a weak; the virtue of the besieged is as great as that of the besiegers. There are some virtues, I confess, which a good man cannot be without, and yet he had rather have no occasion to employ them. If there were any difference, I should prefer the virtues of patience before those of pleasure; for it is braver to break through difficulties than to temper our delights. But though the subject of virtue may possibly be against nature, as to be burnt or wounded, yet the virtue itself of *an invincible patience* is according to nature. We may seem, perhaps, to promise more than human nature is able to perform; but we speak with a respect to the mind, and not to the body.

If a man does not live up to his own rules, it is something yet to have virtuous meditations and good purposes, even without acting; it is generous, the very adventure of being good, and the bare proposal of an eminent course of life, though beyond the force of human frailty to accomplish. There is something of honor yet in the miscarriage; nay, in the naked contemplation of it. I would receive my own death with as little trouble as I would hear of another man's; I would bear the same mind whether I be rich or poor, whether I get or lose in the world; what I have, I will neither sordidly spare, or prodigally squander away, and I will reckon upon benefits well-placed as the fairest part of my possession: not valuing them by number or weight, but by the profit and esteem of the receiver; accounting myself never the poorer for that which I give to a worthy person. What I do shall be done for conscience, not ostentation. I will eat and drink, not to gratify my palate, or only to fill and empty, but to satisfy nature: I will be cheerful to my friends, mild and placable to my enemies: I will prevent an honest request if I can foresee it, and I will grant it without asking: I will look upon the whole world as my country, and upon the gods, both as the witnesses and the judges of my words and deeds. I will live and die with this testimony, that I loved good studies, and a good conscience; that I never invaded another man's liberty; and that I preserved my own. I will govern my life and my thoughts as if the whole world were to see the one, and to read the other; for "what does it signify to make anything a secret to my neighbor, when to God (who is the searcher of our hearts) all our privacies are open?"

Virtue is divided into two parts, *contemplation* and *action*. The one is delivered by institution, the other by admonition: one part of virtue consists in discipline, the other in exercise: for we must first learn, and then practice. The sooner we begin to apply ourselves to it, and the more haste we make, the longer shall we enjoy the comforts of a rectified mind; nay, we have the fruition of it in the very act of forming it: but it is another sort of delight, I must confess, that arises from a contemplation of a soul which is advanced into the possession of wisdom and virtue. If it was so great a comfort to us to pass from the subjection of our childhood into a state of liberty and business, how much greater will it be when we come to cast off the boyish levity of our minds, and range ourselves among the philosophers? We are past our minority, it is true, but not our indiscretions; and, which is yet worse, we have the authority of seniors, and the weaknesses of children, (I might have said of infants, for every little thing frights the one, and every trivial fancy the other.) Whoever studies this point well will find that many things are the less to be feared the more terrible they appear. To think anything good that is not honest, were to reproach Providence; for good men suffer many inconveniences; but virtue, like the sun, goes on still with her work, let the air be never so cloudy, and finishes her course, extinguishing likewise all other splendors and oppositions; insomuch that calamity is no more to a virtuous mind, than a shower into the sea. That which is right, is not to be valued by *quantity, number*, or *time*; a life of a day may be as honest as a life of a hundred years: but yet virtue in one man may have a larger field to show itself in than in another. One man, perhaps, may be in a station to administer unto cities and kingdoms; to contrive good laws, create friendships, and do beneficial offices to mankind.

For virtue is open to all; as well to servants and exiles, as to princes: it is profitable to the world and to itself, at all distances and in all conditions; and there is no difficulty can excuse a man from the exercise of it; and it is only to be found in a wise man, though there may be some faint resemblances of it in the common people. The Stoics hold all virtues to be equal; but yet there is great variety in the matter they have to work upon, according as it is larger or narrower, illustrious or less noble, of more or less extent; as all good men are equal, that is to say, as they are good; but yet one may be young, another old; one may be rich, another poor; one eminent and powerful, another unknown and obscure. There are many things which have little or no grace in themselves, and are yet glorious and remarkable by virtue. Nothing can be good which gives neither greatness nor security to the mind; but, on the contrary, infects it with insolence, arrogance, and tumor: nor does virtue dwell upon the tip of the tongue, but in the temple of a purified heart. He that depends upon any other good becomes covetous of life, and what belongs to it; which exposes a man to appetites that are vast, unlimited, and intolerable. Virtue is free and indefatigable, and accompanied with concord and gracefulness; whereas pleasure is mean, servile, transitory, tiresome, and sickly and scarce outlives the tasting of it: it is the good of the belly, and not of the man; and only the felicity of brutes. Who does not know that fools enjoy their pleasures, and that there is great variety in the entertainments of wickedness? Nay, the mind itself has its variety of perverse pleasures as well as the body: as insolence, self-conceit, pride, garrulity, laziness, and the abusive wit of turning everything into *ridicule*, whereas virtue weighs all this, and corrects it. It is the knowledge both of others and of itself; it is to be learned from itself; and the very will itself may be taught; which will cannot be right, unless the whole habit of the mind be right from whence the will comes. It is by the impulse of virtue that we love virtue, so that the very way to virtue, lies by virtue, which takes in also, at a view, the laws of human life.

Neither are we to value ourselves upon a day, or an hour, or any one action, but upon the whole habit of the mind. Some men do one thing bravely, but not another; they will shrink at infamy, and bear up against poverty: in this case, we commend the fact, and despise the man. The soul is never in the right place until it be delivered from the cares of human affairs; we must labor and climb the hill, if we will arrive at virtue, whose seat is upon the top of it. He that masters avarice, and is truly good, stands firm against ambition; he looks upon his last hour not as a punishment, but as the equity of a common fate; he that subdues his carnal lusts shall easily keep himself untainted with any other: so that reason does not encounter this or that vice by itself, but beats down all at a blow. What does he care for ignominy that only values himself upon conscience, and not opinion? Socrates looked a scandalous death in the face with the same constancy that he had before practiced towards the thirty tyrants: his virtue consecrated the very dungeon: as Cato's repulse was Cato's honor, and the reproach of the government. He that is wise will take delight even in an ill opinion that is well gotten; it is ostentation, not virtue, when a man will have his good deeds published; and it is not enough to be just where there is honor to be gotten, but to continue so, in defiance of infamy and danger.

But virtue cannot lie hid, for the time will come that shall raise it again (even after it is buried) and deliver it from the malignity of the age that oppressed it: immortal glory is the shadow of it, and keeps it company whether we will or not; but sometimes the shadow goes before the substance, and other whiles it follows it; and the later it comes, the larger it is, when even envy itself shall have given way to it. It was a long time that Democritus was taken for a madman, and before Socrates had any esteem in the world. How long was it before Cato could be understood? Nay, he was affronted, contemned, and rejected; and the people never knew the value of him until they had lost him: the integrity and courage of mad Rutilius had been forgotten but for his sufferings. I speak of those that fortune has made famous for their persecutions: and there are others also that the world never took notice of until they were dead; as Epicurus and Metrodorus, that were almost wholly unknown, even in the place where they lived.

Now, as the body is to be kept in upon the down-hill, and forced upwards, so there are some virtues that require the rein and others the spur. In *liberality, temperance, gentleness* of nature, we are to check ourselves for fear of falling; but in *patience, resolutions*, and *perseverance*, where we are to mount the hill, we stand in need of encouragement. Upon this division of the matter, I had rather steer the smoother course than pass through the experiments of sweat and blood: I know it is my duty to be content in all conditions; but yet, if it were at my election, I would choose the fairest. When a man comes once to stand in need of fortune, his life is anxious, suspicious, timorous, dependent upon every moment, and in fear of all accidents. How can that man resign himself to God, or bear his lot, whatever it be, without murmuring, and cheerfully submit to Providence, that shrinks at every motion of pleasure or pain? It is virtue alone that raises us above griefs, hopes, fears and chances; and makes us not only patient, but willing, as knowing that whatever we suffer is according to the decree of Heaven. He that is overcome with pleasure, (so contemptible and weak an enemy) what will become of him when he comes to grapple with dangers, necessities, torments, death, and the dissolution of nature itself? Wealth, honor, and favor, may come upon a man by chance; nay, they may be cast upon him without so much as looking after them: but virtue is the work of industry and labor; and certainly it is worth the while to purchase that good which brings all others along with it. A good man is happy within himself, and independent upon fortune: kind to his friend, temperate to his enemy, religiously just, indefatigably laborious; and he discharges all duties with a constancy and congruity of actions.

CHAPTER IV.
PHILOSOPHY IS THE GUIDE OF LIFE.

If it be true, that the *understanding* and the *will* are the *two eminent faculties of the reasonable soul*, it follows necessarily, that *wisdom* and *virtue*, (which are the best improvements of these two faculties,) must be the perfection also of *our reasonable being*; and consequently, *the undeniable foundation of a happy life*. There is not any duty to which Providence has not annexed a blessing; nor any institution of Heaven which, even in this life, we may not be the better for; not any temptation, either of fortune or of appetite, that is not subject to our reason; nor any passion or affliction for which virtue has not provided a remedy. So that it is our own fault if we either fear or hope for anything; which two affections are the root of all our miseries. From this general prospect of the *foundation* of our *tranquillity*, we shall pass by degrees to a particular consideration of the means by which it may be *procured*, and of the *impediments* that obstruct it; beginning with that *philosophy* which principally regards our manners, and instructs us in the measures of a virtuous and quiet life.

Philosophy is divided into *moral, natural,* and *rational*: the *first* concerns our *manners*; the *second* searches the works of *Nature*; and the *third* furnishes us with propriety of *words* and *arguments*, and the faculty of *distinguishing*, that we may not be imposed upon with tricks and fallacies. The *causes* of things fall under *natural philosophy*, *arguments* under *rational*, and *actions* under *moral*.

Moral philosophy is again divided into matter of *justice*, which arises from the estimation of things and of men; and into *affections* and *actions*; and a failing in any one of these, disorders all the rest: for what does it profit us to know the true value of things, if we be transported by our passion? or to master our appetites without understanding the *when*, the *what*, the *how*, and other circumstances of our proceedings? For it is one thing to know the rate and dignity of things, and another to know the little nicks and springs of acting.

Natural philosophy is conversant about things *corporeal* and *incorporeal*; the disquisition of *causes* and *effects*, and the contemplation of the *cause of causes*.

Rational philosophy is divided into *logic* and *rhetoric*; the one looks after *words, sense,* and *order*; the other treats barely of *words*, and the *significations* of them.

Socrates places all *philosophy* in *morals*; and *wisdom* in the distinguishing of *good* and *evil*. It is the art and law of life, and it teaches us what to do in all cases, and, like good marksmen, to hit the white at any distance. The force of it is incredible; for it gives us in the weakness of a man the security of a *spirit*: in sickness it is as good as a remedy to us; for whatsoever eases the mind is profitable also to the body. The *physician* may prescribe diet and exercise, and accommodate his rule and medicine to the disease, but it is *philosophy* that must bring us to a contempt of death, which is the remedy of all diseases. In poverty it gives us riches, or such a state of mind as makes them superfluous to us. It arms us against all difficulties: one man is pressed with death, another with poverty; some with envy, others are offended at Providence, and unsatisfied with the condition of mankind: but *philosophy* prompts us to relieve the prisoner, the infirm, the necessitous, the condemned; to show the ignorant their errors, and rectify their affections. It makes us inspect and govern our manners; it rouses us where we are faint and drowsy: it binds up what is loose, and humbles in us that which is contumacious: it delivers the mind from the bondage of the body, and raises it up to the contemplation of its divine original. Honors, monuments, and all the works of vanity and ambition are demolished and destroyed by time; but the reputation of wisdom is venerable to posterity, and those that were envied or neglected in their lives are adored in their memories, and exempted from the very laws of created nature, which has set bounds to all other things. The very shadow of *glory* carries a man of *honor* upon all dangers, to the contempt of fire and sword; and it were a shame if *right reason* should not inspire as generous resolutions into a man of *virtue*.

Neither is *philosophy* only profitable to the public, but one wise man helps another, even in the exercise of the virtues; and the one has need of the other, both for conversation and counsel; for they kindle a mutual emulation in good offices. We are not so perfect yet, but that many new things remain still to be found out, which will give us the reciprocal advantages of instructing one another: for as one wicked man is contagious to another, and the more vices are mingled, the worse it is, so is it on the contrary with good men and their virtues. As men of letters are the most useful and excellent of friends, so are they the best of subjects; as being better judges of the blessings they enjoy under a well-ordered government, and of what they owe to the magistrate for their freedom and protection. They are men of sobriety and learning, and free from boasting and insolence; they reprove the vice without reproaching the person; for they have learned to be without either pomp or envy. That which we see in high mountains, we find in *philosophers*; they seem taller near at hand than at a distance. They are raised above other men, but their greatness is substantial. Nor do they stand upon tiptoe, that they may seem higher than they are, but, content with their own stature, they reckon themselves tall enough when fortune cannot reach them. Their laws are short, and yet comprehensive too, for they bind all.

It is the bounty of *nature* that we *live*; but of *philosophy* that we *live well*, which is in truth a greater benefit than life itself. Not but that *philosophy* is also the gift of Heaven, so far as to the faculty, but not to the science; for that must be the business of industry. No man is born wise; but wisdom and virtue require a tutor, though we can easily learn to be vicious without a master. It is *philosophy* that gives us a veneration for God, a charity for our neighbor, that teaches us our duty to Heaven, and exhorts us to an agreement one with another; it unmasks things that are terrible to us, assuages our lusts, refutes our errors, restrains our luxury, reproves our avarice, and works strangely upon tender natures. I could never hear Attalus (says Seneca) upon the vices of the age and the errors of life, without a compassion for mankind; and in his discourses upon poverty, there was something methought that was more than human. "More than we use," says he, "is more than we need, and only a burden to the bearer." That saying of his put me out of countenance at the superfluities of my own fortune. And so in his invectives against vain pleasures, he did at such a rate advance the felicities of a sober table, a pure mind, and a chaste body that a man could not hear him without a love for continence and moderation. Upon these lectures of his, I denied myself, for a while after, certain delicacies that I had formerly used: but in a short time I fell to them again, though so sparingly, that the proportion came little short of a total abstinence.

Now, to show you (says our author) how much earnester my entrance upon philosophy was than my progress, my tutor Sotion gave me a wonderful kindness for Pythagoras, and after him for Sextius: the former forbore shedding of blood upon his *metempsychosis*: and put men in fear of it, lest they should offer violence to the souls of some of their departed friends or relations. "Whether," says he, "there be a transmigration or not; if it be true, there is no hurt; if false, there is frugality: and nothing is gotten by cruelty neither, but the cozening a wolf, perhaps, or a vulture, of a supper."

Now, Sextius abstained upon another account, which was, that he would not have men inured to hardness of heart by the laceration and tormenting of living creatures; beside, "that Nature had sufficiently provided for the sustenance of mankind without blood." This wrought upon me so far that I gave over eating of flesh, and in one year I made it not only easy to me but pleasant; my mind methought was more at liberty, (and I am still of the same opinion,) but I gave it over nevertheless; and the reason was this: it was imputed as a superstition to the Jews, the forbearance of some sorts of flesh, and my father brought me back again to my old custom, that I might not be thought tainted with their superstition. Nay, and I had much ado to prevail upon myself to suffer it too. I make use of this instance to show the aptness of youth to take good impressions, if there be a friend at hand to press them.

Philosophers are the tutors of mankind; if they have found out remedies for the mind, it must be our part to employ them. I cannot think of Cato, Lelius, Socrates, Plato, without veneration: their very names are sacred to me. Philosophy is the health of the mind; let us look to that health first, and in the second place to that of the body, which may be had upon easier terms; for a strong arm, a robust constitution, or the skill of procuring this, is not a philosopher's business. He does some things as a *wise man*, and other things as he is a *man*; and he may have strength of body as well as of mind; but if he runs, or casts the sledge, it were injurious to ascribe that to his wisdom which is common to the greatest of fools.

He studies rather to fill his mind than his coffers; and he knows that gold and silver were mingled with dirt, until avarice or ambition parted them. His life is ordinate, fearless, equal, secure; he stands firm in all extremities, and bears the lot of his humanity with a divine temper. There is a great difference betwixt the splendor of philosophy and of fortune; the one shines with an original light, the other with a borrowed one; beside that it makes us happy and immortal: for learning shall outlive palaces and monuments.

The house of a wise man is safe, though narrow; there is neither noise nor furniture in it, no porter at the door, nor anything that is either vendible or mercenary, nor any business of fortune, for she has nothing to do where she has nothing to look after. This is the way to Heaven which Nature has chalked out, and it is both secure and pleasant; there needs no train of servants, no pomp or equipage, to make good our passage; no money or letters of credit, for expenses upon the voyage; but the graces of an honest mind will serve us upon the way, and make us happy at our journey's end.

To tell you my opinion now of the *liberal sciences*; I have no great esteem for any thing that terminates in profit or money; and yet I shall allow them to be so far beneficial, as they only prepare the understanding without *detaining* it. They are but the rudiments of wisdom, and only then to be learned when the mind is capable of nothing better, and the knowledge of them is better worth the keeping than the acquiring. They do not so much as pretend to the making of us virtuous, but only to give us an aptitude of disposition to be so. The *grammarian's* business lies in a syntax of speech; or if he proceed to *history*, or the measuring of a *verse*, he is at the end of his line; but what signifies a congruity of periods, the computing of syllables, or the modifying of numbers, to the taming of our passions, or the repressing of our lusts? The *philosopher* proves the body of the sun to be large, but for the true dimensions of it we must ask the *mathematician*: geometry and *music*, if they do not teach us to master our hopes and fears, all the rest is to little purpose.

What does it concern us which was the elder of the two, Homer or Hesiod? or which was the taller, Helen or Hecuba? We take a great deal of pains to trace Ulysses in his wanderings, but were it not time as well spent to look to ourselves that we may not wander at all? Are not we ourselves tossed with tempestuous passions? and both *assaulted* by terrible *monsters* on the one hand, and *tempted* by syrens on the other? Teach me my duty to my country, to my father, to my wife, to mankind. What is it to me whether Penelope was honest or not? teach me to know how to be so myself, and to live according to that knowledge. What am I the better for putting so many parts together in music, and raising a harmony out of so many different tones? teach me to tune my affections, and to hold constant to myself. *Geometry* teaches me the art of *measuring* acres; teach me to *measure my appetites*, and to know when I have enough; teach me to divide with my brother, and to rejoice in the prosperity of my neighbor. You teach me how I may hold my own, and keep my estate; but I would rather learn how I may lose it all, and yet be contented. "It is hard," you will say, "for a man to be forced from the fortune of his family." This estate, it is true, was my father's; but whose was it in the time of my grandfather? I do not only say, what *man's* was it? but what *nation's*? The *astrologer* tells me of Saturn and Mars in *opposition*; but I say, let them be as they will, their courses and their positions are ordered them by an unchangeable decree of fate. Either they produce and point out the effects of all things, or else they signify them; if the former, what are we the better for the knowledge of that which must of necessity come to pass? If the latter, what does it avail us to foresee what we cannot avoid? So that whether we know or not know, the event will still be the same.

He that designs the institution of human life should not be over-curious of his words; it does not stand with his dignity to be solicitous about sounds and syllables, and to debase the mind of man with trivial things; placing wisdom in matters that are rather difficult than great. If it be eloquent, it is his *good fortune*, not his *business*. Subtle disputations are only the sport of wits, that play upon the catch, and are fitter to be contemned than resolved. Were not I a madman to sit wrangling about words, and putting of nice and impertinent questions, when the enemy has already made the breach, the town fired over my head, and the mine ready to play that shall blow me up into the air? were this a time for fooleries?

Let me rather fortify myself against death and inevitable necessities; let me understand that the good of life does not consist in the length or space, but in the use of it. When I go to sleep, who knows whether I shall ever wake again? and when I wake, whether ever I shall sleep again? When I go abroad, whether ever I shall come home again? and when I return, whether ever I shall go abroad again? It is not at sea only that life and death are within a few inches one of another; but they are as near everywhere else too, only we do not take so much notice of it. What have we to do with frivolous and captious questions, and impertinent niceties? Let us rather study how to deliver ourselves from sadness, fear, and the burden of all our secret lusts: let us pass over all our most solemn levities, and make haste to a good life, which is a thing that presses us. Shall a man that goes for a *midwife*, stand gaping upon a post to see *what play to-day*? or, when his house is on fire, stay the curling of a periwig before he calls for help? Our houses are on fire, our country invaded, our goods taken away, our children in danger; and, I might add to these, the calamities of earthquakes, shipwrecks, and whatever else is most terrible. Is this a time for us now to be playing fast and loose with idle questions, which are in effect so many unprofitable riddles?

Our duty is the cure of the mind rather than the delight of it; but we have only the words of wisdom without the works; and turn philosophy into a pleasure that was given for a remedy. What can be more ridiculous than for a man to neglect his *manners* and compose his *style*? We are sick and ulcerous, and must be lanced and scarified, and every man has as much business within himself as a physician in a common pestilence. "Misfortunes," in fine, "cannot be avoided; but they may be sweetened, if not overcome; and our lives may be made happy by philosophy."

CHAPTER V.
THE FORCE OF PRECEPTS.

There seems to be so near an affinity betwixt *wisdom, philosophy,* and *good counsels*, that it is rather a matter of curiosity than of profit to divide them; *philosophy*, being only a *limited wisdom*; and *good counsels* a communication of that wisdom, for the good of others, as well as of ourselves; and to posterity, as well as to the present. The *wisdom of the ancients*, as to the government of life, was no more than certain precepts, what to do and what not: and men were much better in that simplicity; for as they came to be more *learned*, they grew less careful of being *good*. That plain and open virtue is now turned into a dark and intricate science; and we are taught to *dispute* rather than to *live*. So long as wickedness was simple, simple remedies also were sufficient against it; but now it has taken root, and spread, we must make use of stronger.

There are some dispositions that embrace good things as soon as they hear them; but they will still need quickening by admonition and precept. We are rash and forward in some cases, and dull in others; and there is no repressing of the one humor, or raising of the other, but by removing the causes of them; which are (in one word) *false admiration* and *false fear*.

Every man knows his duty to his country, to his friends, to his guests; and yet when he is called upon to draw his sword for the one, or to labor for the other, he finds himself distracted betwixt his apprehensions and his delights: he knows well enough the injury he does his wife in the keeping of a wench, and yet his lust overrules him: so that it is not enough to give good advice, unless we can take away that which hinders the benefit of it. If a man does what he ought to do, he will never do it constantly or equally, without knowing why he does it: and if it be only chance or custom, he that does well by chance, may do ill so too. And farther, a precept may direct us what we *ought* to do, and yet fall short in the manner of doing it: an expensive entertainment may, in one case be extravagance or gluttony, and yet a point of honor and discretion in another. Tiberius Cæsar had a huge mullet presented him, which he sent to the market to be sold: "and now," says he, "my masters," to some company with him, "you shall see that either Apicius or Octavius will be the chapman for this fish." Octavius beat the price, and gave about thirty pounds sterling for it. Now, there was a great difference between Octavius, that bought it for his luxury, and the other that purchased it for a *compliment* to Tiberius.

Precepts are idle, if we be not first taught what opinion we are to have of the matter in question; whether it be *poverty, riches, disgrace, sickness, banishment,* etc. Let us therefore examine them one by one; not what they are *called*, but what in truth they are. And so for the virtues; it is to no purpose to set a high esteem upon *prudence, fortitude, temperance, justice,* if we do not first know *what virtue is*; whether one or more; or if he that has *one*, has *all*; or *how they differ.*

Precepts are of great weight; and a few useful ones at hand do more toward a happy life than whole volumes or cautions, that we know not where to find. These salutary precepts should be our daily meditation, for they are the rules by which we ought to square our lives. When they are contracted into sentences, they strike the affections: whereas admonition is only blowing of the coal; it moves the vigor of the mind, and excites virtue: we have the thing already, but we know not where it lies. It is by precept that the understanding is nourished and augmented: the offices of prudence and justice are guided by them, and they lead us to the execution of our duties.

A precept delivered in *verse* has a much greater effect than in prose: and those very people that never think they have enough, let them but hear a sharp sentence against avarice, how will they clap and admire it, and bid open defiance to money? So soon as we find the affections struck, we must follow the blow; not with *syllogisms* or quirks of *wit*; but with *plain* and *weighty reason* and we must do it with *kindness* too, and *respect* for "there goes a blessing along with counsels and discourses that are bent wholly upon the good of the hearer:" and those are still the most efficacious that take reason along with them; and tell us as well *why* we are to do this or that, as *what* we are to do: for some understandings are weak, and need an instructor to expound to them what is good and what is evil. It is a great virtue to *love*, to *give*, and to *follow good counsel*; if it does not lead us to honesty, it does at least *prompt* us to it.

As several parts make up but one harmony, and the most agreeable music arises from discords; so should a wise man gather many acts, many precepts, and the examples of many arts, to inform his own life. Our forefathers have left us in charge to avoid three things; *hatred, envy,* and *contempt*; now, it is hard to avoid envy and not incur contempt; for in taking too much care not to usurp upon others, we become many times liable to be trampled upon ourselves. Some people are afraid of others, because it is possible that others may be afraid of them: but let us secure ourselves upon all hands; for *flattery* is as dangerous as contempt. It is not to say, in case of admonition, I knew this before, for we know many things, but we do not think of them; so that it is the part of a *monitor*, not so much to *teach* as to *mind* us of our duties. Sometimes a man oversees that which lies just under his nose; otherwhile he is careless, or *pretends* not to see it: we do all know that friendship is sacred, and yet we violate it; and the greatest libertine expects that his own wife should be honest.

Good counsel is the most needful service that we can do to mankind; and if we give it to *many*, it will be sure to profit *some*: for of many trials, some or other will undoubtedly succeed. He that places a man in the possession of himself does a great thing; for wisdom does not show itself so much in precept as in life; in a firmness of mind and a mastery of appetite: it teaches us to *do* as well as to *talk*:

and to make our words and actions all of a color. If that fruit be pleasantest which we gather from a tree of our own planting, how much greater delight shall we take in the growth and increase of good manners of our own forming! It is an eminent mark of wisdom for a man to be always like himself. You shall have some that keep a thrifty table, and lavish out upon building; profuse upon themselves, and forbid to others; niggardly at home, and lavish abroad. This diversity is vicious, and the effect of a dissatisfied and uneasy mind; whereas every wise man lives by rule. This disagreement of purposes arises from hence, either that we do not propound to ourselves what we would be at; or if we do, that we do not pursue it, but pass from one thing to another; and we do not only change neither but return to the very thing which we had both quitted and condemned.

In all our undertakings, let us first examine our own strength; the enterprise next; and, thirdly, the persons with whom we have to do.

The first point is most important; for we are apt to overvalue ourselves, and reckon that we can do more than indeed we can. One man sets up for a speaker, and is out as soon as he opens his mouth; another overcharges his estate, perhaps, or his body: a bashful man is not fit for public business: some again are too stiff and peremptory for the court: many people are apt to fly out in their anger, nay, and in a frolic too; if any sharp thing fall in their way, they will rather venture a neck than lose a jest. These people had better be quiet in the world than busy. Let him that is naturally choleric and impatient avoid all provocations, and those affairs also that multiply and draw on more; and those also from which there is no retreat. When we may come off at pleasure, and fairly hope to bring our matters to a period, it is well enough. If it so happen that a man be tied up to business, which he can neither loosen nor break off, let him imagine those shackles upon his mind to be irons upon his legs: they are troublesome at first; but when there is no remedy but patience, custom makes them easy to us, and necessity gives us courage.

We are all slaves to fortune: some only in loose and golden chains, others in strait ones, and coarser: nay, and *they that bind us are slaves themselves also*; some to honor, others to wealth; some to offices, and others to contempt; some to their superiors, others to themselves: nay, life itself is a servitude: let us make the best of it then, and with our philosophy mend our fortune. Difficulties may be softened, and heavy burdens disposed of to our ease. Let us covet nothing out of our reach, but content ourselves with things hopeful and at hand; and without envying the advantages of others; for greatness stands upon a craggy precipice, and it is much safer and quieter living upon a level. How many great men are forced to keep their station upon mere necessity; because they find there is no coming down from it but headlong? These men should do well to fortify themselves against ill consequences by such virtues and meditations as may make them less solicitous for the future. The surest expedient in this case is to bound our desires, and to leave nothing to fortune which we may keep in our own power. Neither will this course wholly compose us, but it shows us at worst the end of our troubles.

It is but a main point to take care that we propose nothing but what is hopeful and honest. For it will be equally troublesome to us, either not to succeed, or to be ashamed of the success. Wherefore let us be sure not to admit any ill design into our heart; that we may lift up pure hands to heaven and ask nothing which another shall be a loser by. Let us pray for a good mind, which is a wish to no man's injury. I will remember always that I am a man, and then consider, that if I am *happy,* it will not last *always*; if *unhappy*, I may be *other* if I please. I will carry my life in my hand, and deliver it up readily when it shall be called for. I will have a care of being a slave to myself; for it is a perpetual, a shameful, and the heaviest of all servitudes: and this may be done by moderate desires. I will say to myself, "What is it that I labor, sweat, and solicit for, when it is but very little that I want, and it will not be long that I will need any thing?" He that would make a trial of the firmness of his mind, let him set certain days apart for the practice of his virtues. Let him mortify himself with fasting, coarse clothes, and hard lodging; and then say to himself, "Is this the thing now that I was afraid of?" In a state of security, a man may thus prepare himself against hazards, and in plenty fortify himself against want. If you will have a man resolute when he comes to the push, train him up to it beforehand. The soldier does duty in peace, that he may be in breath when he comes to battle. How many great and wise men have made experiment of their moderation by a practice of abstinence, to the highest degree of hunger and thirst; and convinced themselves that a man may fill his belly without being beholden to fortune; which never denies any of us wherewith to satisfy our necessities, though she be never so angry! It is as easy to *suffer* it *always* as to *try it once*; and it is no more than thousands of servants and poor people do every day in their lives.

He that would live happily, must neither trust to good fortune nor submit to bad: he must stand upon his guard against all assaults; he must stick to himself, without any dependence upon other people. Where the mind is tinctured with philosophy, there is no place for grief, anxiety, or superfluous vexations. It is prepossessed with virtue to the neglect of fortune, which brings us to a degree of security not to be disturbed. It is easier to give counsel than to take it; and a common thing for one choleric man to condemn another. We may be sometimes earnest in advising, but not violent or tedious. Few words, with gentleness and efficacy, are best: the misery is, that the wise do not need counsel, and fools will not take it. A good man, it is true, delights in it; and it is a mark of folly and ill-nature to hate reproof.

To a friend I would be always frank and plain; and rather fail in the success than be wanting in the matter of faith and trust. There are some precepts that serve in common both to the rich and poor, but they are too general; as "Cure your avarice, and the work is done." It is one thing not to desire money, and another thing not to understand how to use it. In the choice of the persons we have to do withal, we should see that they be worth our while; in the choice of our business, we are to consult nature, and follow our inclinations. He that gives sober advice to a witty droll must look to have every thing turned into ridicule. "As if you philosophers," says Marcellinus, "did not love your whores and your guts as well as other people:" and then he tells you of such and such that were taken in the manner. We are all sick, I must confess, and it is not for sick men to play the physicians; but it is yet lawful for a man in an hospital to discourse of the common condition and distempers of the place. He that should pretend to teach a madman how to speak, walk, and behave himself, were not he the most mad man of the two? He that directs the pilot, makes him move the helm, order the sails so or so, and makes the best of a scant wind, after this or that manner. And so should we do in our counsels.

Do not tell me what a man should do in health or poverty, but show me the way to be either sound or rich. Teach me to master my vices: for it is to no purpose, so long as I am under their government, to tell me what I must do when I am clear of it. In case of an avarice a little eased, a luxury moderated, a temerity restrained, a sluggish humor quickened; precepts will then help us forward, and tutor us how to behave ourselves. It is the first and the main tie of a soldier his military oath, which is an engagement upon him both of religion and honor. In like manner, he that pretends to a happy life must first lay a foundation of virtue, as a bond upon him, to live and die true to that cause. We do not find felicity in the veins of the earth where we dig for gold, nor in the bottom of the sea where we fish for pearls, but in a pure and untainted mind, which, if it were not holy, were not fit to entertain the Deity. "He that would be truly happy, must think his own lot best, and so live with men, as considering that God sees him, and so speak to God as if men heard him."

CHAPTER VI.
NO FELICITY LIKE PEACE OF CONSCIENCE.

"A good conscience is the testimony of a good life, and the reward of it." This is it that fortifies the mind against fortune, when a man has gotten the mastery of his passions; placed his treasure and security within himself; learned to be content with his condition; and that death is no evil in itself, but only the end of man. He that has dedicated his mind to virtue, and to the good of human society, whereof he is a member, has consummated all that is either profitable or necessary for him to know or to do toward the establishment of his peace. Every man has a judge and a witness within himself of all the good and ill that he does, which inspires us with great thoughts, and administers to us wholesome counsels. We have a veneration for all the works of Nature, the heads of rivers, and the springs of medicinal waters; the horrors of groves and of caves strike us with an impression of religion and worship. To see a man fearless in dangers, untainted with lusts, happy in adversity, composed in a tumult, and laughing at all those things which are generally either coveted or feared; all men must acknowledge that this can be nothing else but a beam of divinity that influences a mortal body. And this is it that carries us to the disquisition of things divine and human; what the state of the world was before the distribution of the first matter into parts; what power it was that drew order out of that confusion, and gave laws both to the whole, and to every particle thereof; what that space is beyond the world; and whence proceed the several operations of Nature.

Shall any man see the glory and order of the universe; so many scattered parts and qualities wrought into one mass; such a medley of things, which are yet distinguished: the world enlightened, and the disorders of it so wonderfully regulated; and shall he not consider the Author and Disposer of all this; and whither we ourselves shall go, when our souls shall be delivered from the slavery of our flesh? The whole creation we see conforms to the dictates of Providence, and follows God both as a governor and as a guide. A great, a good, and a right mind, is a kind of divinity lodged in flesh, and may be the blessing of a slave as well as of a prince; it came from heaven, and to heaven it must return; and it is a kind of heavenly felicity, which a pure and virtuous mind enjoys, in some degree, even upon earth: whereas temples of honor are but empty names, which, probably, owe their beginning either to ambition or to violence.

I am strangely transported with the thoughts of eternity; nay, with the belief of it; for I have a profound veneration for the opinions of great men, especially when they promise things so much to my satisfaction: for they do promise them, though they do not prove them. In the question of the immortality of the soul, it goes very far with me, a general consent to the opinion of a future reward and punishment; which meditation raises me to the contempt of this life, in hopes of a better. But still, though we know that we have a soul; yet what the soul is, how, and from whence, we are utterly ignorant: this only we understand, that all the good and ill we do is under the dominion of the mind; that a clear conscience states us in an inviolable peace; and that the greatest blessing in Nature is that which every honest man may bestow upon himself. The body is but the clog and prisoner of the mind; tossed up and down, and persecuted with punishments, violences, and diseases; but the mind itself is sacred and eternal, and exempt from the danger of all actual impression.

Provided that we look to our consciences, no matter for opinion: let me deserve well, though I hear ill. The common people take stomach and audacity for the marks of magnanimity and honor; and if a man be soft and modest, they look upon him as an easy fop; but when they come once to observe the dignity of his mind in the equality and firmness of his actions; and that his external quiet is founded upon an internal peace, the very same people have him in esteem and admiration; for there is no man but approves of virtue, though but few pursue it; we see where it is, but we dare not venture to come at it: and the reason is, we overvalue that which we must quit to obtain it.

A good conscience fears no witnesses, but a guilty conscience is solicitous even of solitude. If we do nothing but what is honest, let all the world know it; but if otherwise, what does it signify to have nobody else know it, so long as I know it myself? Miserable is he that slights that witness! Wickedness, it is true, may escape the law, but not the conscience; for a private conviction is the first and the greatest punishment to offenders; so that sin plagues itself; and the fear of vengeance pursues even those that escape the stroke of it. It were ill for good men that iniquity may so easily evade the law, the judge, and the execution, if Nature had not set up torments and gibbets in the consciences of transgressors. He that is guilty lives in perpetual terror; and while he expects to be punished, he punishes himself; and whosoever deserves it expects it. What if he be not detected? he is still in apprehension yet that he may be so. His sleeps are painful, and never secure; and he cannot speak of another man's wickedness without thinking of his own, whereas a good conscience is a continual feast.

Those are the only certain and profitable delights, which arise from the consciousness of a well-acted life; no matter for noise abroad, so long as we are quiet within: but if our passions be seditious, that is enough to keep us waking without any other tumult. It is not the posture of the body, or the composure of the bed, that will give rest to an uneasy mind: there is an impatient sloth that may be roused by action, and the vices of laziness must be cured by business. True happiness is not to be found in excesses of wine, or of women, or in the largest prodigalities of fortune; what she has given to me, she may take away, but she shall not tear it from me; and, so long as it does not grow to me, I can part with it without pain. He that would perfectly know himself, let him set aside his money, his fortune, his dignity, and examine himself naked, without being put to learn from others the knowledge of himself.

It is dangerous for a man too suddenly, or too easily, to believe himself. Wherefore let us examine, observe, and inspect our own hearts, for we ourselves are our own greatest flatterers: we should every night call ourselves to account, "What infirmity have I mastered to-day? what passion opposed? what temptation resisted? what virtue acquired?" Our vices will abate of themselves, if they be brought every day to the shrift. Oh the blessed sleep that follows such a diary! Oh the tranquillity, liberty, and greatness of that mind that is a spy upon itself, and a private censor of its own manners! It is my custom (says our author) every night, so soon as the candle is out, to run over all the words and actions of the past day; and I let nothing escape me; for why should I fear the sight of my own errors, when I can admonish and forgive myself ? "I was a little too hot in such a dispute: my opinion might have been as well spared, for it gave offence, and did no good at all. The thing was true, but all truths are not to be spoken at all times; I would I had held my tongue, for there is no contending either with fools or our superiors. I have done ill, but it shall be so no more." If every man would but thus look into himself, it would be the better for us all. What can be more reasonable than this daily review of a life that we cannot warrant for a moment? Our fate is set, and the first breath we draw is only the first motion toward our last: one cause depends upon another; and the course of all things, public and private, is but a long connection of providential appointments. There is a great variety in our lives, but all tends to the same issue. Nature may use her own bodies as she pleases; but a good man has this consolation, that nothing perishes which he can call his own. It is a great comfort that we are only condemned to the same fate with the universe; the heavens themselves are mortal as well as our bodies; Nature has made us passive, and to suffer is our lot. While we are in flesh, every man has his chain and his clog, only it is looser and lighter to one man than to another; and he is more at ease that takes it up and carries it, than he that drags it. We are born, to lose and to perish, to hope and to fear, to vex ourselves and others; and there is no antidote against a common calamity but virtue; for "the foundation of true joy is in the conscience."

CHAPTER VII.
A GOOD MAN CAN NEVER BE MISERABLE,
NOR A WICKED MAN HAPPY.

There is not in the scale of nature a more inseparable connection of cause and effect, than in the case of happiness and virtue; nor anything that more naturally produces the one, or more necessarily presupposes the other. For what is it to be happy, but for a man to content himself with his lot, in a cheerful and quiet resignation to the appointments of God? All the actions of our lives ought to be governed with respect to good and evil: and it is only reason that distinguishes; by which reason we are in such manner influenced, as if a ray of the Divinity were dipt in a mortal body, and that is the perfection of mankind. It is true, we have not the eyes of eagles or the sagacity of hounds: nor if we had, could we pretend to value ourselves upon anything which we have in common with brutes. What are we the better for that which is foreign to us, and may be given and taken away? As the beams of the sun irradiate the earth, and yet remain where they were; so is it in some proportion with a holy mind that illustrates all our actions, and yet it adheres to its original. Why do we not as well commend a horse for his glorious trappings, as a man for his pompous additions? How much a braver creature is a lion, (which by nature ought to be fierce and terrible) how much braver (I say) in his natural horror than in his chains? so that everything in its pure nature pleases us best. It is not health, nobility, riches, that can justify a wicked man: nor is it the want of all these that can discredit a good one. That is the sovereign blessing, which makes the possessor of it valuable without anything else, and him that wants it contemptible, though he had all the world besides. It is not the painting, gilding, or carving, that makes a good ship; but if she be a nimble sailer, tight and strong to endure the seas; that is her excellency. It is the edge and temper of the blade that makes a good sword, not the richness of the scabbard: and so it is not money or possessions, that makes a man considerable, but his virtue.

It is every man's duty to make himself profitable to mankind – if he can, to many – if not, to fewer – if not so neither, to his neighbor – but, however, to himself. There are two republics: a great one, which is human nature; and a less, which is the place where we were born. Some serve both at a time, some only the greater, and some again only the less. The greater may be served in privacy, solitude, contemplation, and perchance that way better than any other; but it was the intent of Nature, however, that we should serve both. A good man may serve the public, his friend, and himself in any station: if he be not for the sword, let him take the gown; if the bar does not agree with him, let him try the pulpit; if he be silenced abroad, let him give counsel at home, and discharge the part of a faithful friend and a temperate companion. When he is no longer a citizen, he is yet a man; but the whole world is his country, and human nature never wants matter to work upon: but if nothing will serve a man in the *civil government* unless he be *prime minister*, or in the *field* but to *command in chief*, it is his own fault.

The common soldier where he cannot use his hands, fights with his looks, his example, his encouragement, his voice, and stands his ground even when he has lost his hands, and does service too with his very clamor, so that in any condition whatsoever, he still discharges the duty of a good patriot – nay, he that spends his time well even in a retirement, gives a great example.

We may enlarge, indeed, or contract, according to the circumstances of time, place, or abilities; but above all things we must be sure to keep ourselves in action, for he that is slothful is dead even while he lives. Was there ever any state so desperate as that of Athens under the thirty tyrants – where it was capital to be honest, and the senate-house was turned into a college of hangmen? Never was any government so wretched and so hopeless; and yet Socrates at the same time preached *temperance* to the *tyrants*, and courage to the rest, and afterwards died an eminent example of faith and resolution, and a sacrifice for the common good.

It is not for a wise man to stand shifting and fencing with fortune, but to oppose her barefaced, for he is sufficiently convinced that she can do him no hurt; she may take away his servants, possessions, dignity, assault his body, put out his eyes, cut off his hands, and strip him of all the external comforts of life. But what does all this amount to more than the recalling of a trust which he has received, with condition to deliver it up again upon demand? He looks upon himself as precarious, and only lent to himself, and yet he does not value himself ever the less because he is not his own, but takes such care as an honest man should do of a thing that is committed to him in trust. Whensoever he that lent me myself and what I have, shall call for all back again, it is not a loss but a restitution, and I must willingly deliver up what most undeservedly was bestowed upon me, and it will become me to return my mind better than I received it.

Demetrius, upon the taking of Megara, asked Stilpo, the philosopher, what he had lost. "Nothing," said he, "for I had all that I could call my own about me." And yet the enemy had then made himself master of his patrimony, his children, and his country; but these he looked upon as only adventitious goods, and under the command of fortune. Now, he that neither lost any thing nor feared any thing in a public ruin, but was safe and at peace in the middle of the flames, and in the heat of a military intemperance and fury – what violence or provocation imaginable can put such a man as this out of the possession of himself? Walls and castles may be mined and battered, but there is no art or engine that can subvert a steady mind. "I have made my way," says Stilpo, "through fire and blood – what has become of my children I know not; but these are transitory blessings, and servants that are bound to change their masters; what was my own before is my own still. Some have lost their estates, others their dear-bought mistresses, their commissions and offices: the usurers have lost their bonds and securities: but, Demetrius, for my part I have saved all, and do not imagine after all this, either that Demetrius is a conqueror, or that Stilpo is overcome – it is only thy fortune has been too hard for mine."

Alexander took Babylon, Scipio took Carthage, the capitol was burnt; but there is no fire or violence that can discompose a generous mind; and let us not take this character either for a chimera, for all ages afford some, though not many, instances of this elevated virtue.

A good man does his duty, let it be never so painful, so hazardous, or never so great a loss to him; and it is not all the money, the power, and the pleasure in the world; not any force of necessity, that can make him wicked: he considers what he is to do, not what he is to suffer, and will keep on his course, though there should be nothing but gibbets and torments in the way. And in this instance of Stilpo, who, when he had lost his country, his wife, his children, the town on fire over his head, himself escaping very hardly and naked out of the flames; "I have saved all my goods," says he, "my justice, my courage, my temperance, my prudence;" accounting nothing his own, or valuable, and showing how much easier it was to overcome a nation than one wise man. It is a certain mark of a brave mind not to be moved by any accidents: the upper region of the air admits neither clouds nor tempests; the thunder, storms, and meteors, are formed below; and this is the difference betwixt a mean and an exalted mind; the former is rude and tumultuary; the latter is modest, venerable, composed, and always quiet in its station. In brief, it is the conscience that pronounces upon the man whether he be happy or miserable. But, though sacrilege and adultery be generally condemned, how many are there still that do not so much as blush at the one, and in truth that take a glory in the other? For nothing is more common than for great thieves to ride in triumph when the little ones are punished. But let "wickedness escape as it may at the bar, it never fails of doing justice upon itself; for every guilty person is his own hangman."

CHAPTER VIII.
THE DUE CONTEMPLATION OF DIVINE PROVIDENCE IS THE CERTAIN CURE OF ALL MISFORTUNES.

Whoever observes the world, and the order of it, will find all the motions in it to be only vicissitudes of falling and rising; nothing extinguished, and even those things which seem to us to perish are in truth but changed. The seasons go and return, day and night follow in their courses, the heavens roll, and Nature goes on with her work: all things succeed in their turns, storms and calms; the law of Nature will have it so, which we must follow and obey, accounting all things that are done to be well done; so that what we cannot mend we must suffer, and wait upon Providence without repining. It is the part of a cowardly soldier to follow his commander groaning: but a generous man delivers himself up to God without struggling; and it is only for a narrow mind to condemn the order of the world, and to propound rather the mending of Nature than of himself. No man has any cause of complaint against Providence, if that which is right pleases him. Those glories that appear fair to the eye, their lustre is but false and superficial; and they are only vanity and delusion: they are rather the goods of a dream than a substantial possession: they may cozen us at a distance, but bring them once to the touch, they are rotten and counterfeit. There are no greater wretches in the world than many of those which the people take to be happy. Those are the only true and incorruptible comforts that will abide all trials, and the more we turn and examine them, the more valuable we find them; and the greatest felicity of all is, not to stand in need of any. What is *poverty*? No man lives so poor as he was born. What is *pain*? It will either have an end itself, or make an end of us. In short, Fortune has no weapon that reaches the mind: but the bounties of Providence are certain and permanent blessings; and they are the greater and the better, the longer we consider them; that is to say, "the power of contemning things terrible, and despising what the common people covet." In the very methods of Nature we cannot but observe the regard that Providence had to the good of mankind, even in the disposition of the world, in providing so amply for our maintenance and satisfaction. It is not possible for us to comprehend what the Power is which has made all things: some few sparks of that Divinity are discovered, but infinitely the greater part of it lies hid. We are all of us, however, thus far agreed, first, in the acknowledgement and belief of that almighty Being; and, secondly, that we are to ascribe to it all majesty and goodness.

"If there be a Providence," say some, "how comes it to pass that good men labor under affliction and adversity, and wicked men enjoy themselves in ease and plenty?" My answer is, that God deals by us as a good father does by his children; he tries us, he hardens us, and fits us for himself. He keeps a strict hand over those that he loves; and by the rest he does as we do by our slaves; he lets them go on in license and boldness.

As the master gives his most hopeful scholars the hardest lessons, so does God deal with the most generous spirits; and the cross encounters of fortune we are not to look upon as a cruelty, but as a contest: the familiarity of dangers brings us to the contempt of them, and that part is strongest which is most exercised: the seaman's hand is callous, the soldier's arm is strong, and the tree that is most exposed to the wind takes the best root: there are people that live in a perpetual winter, in extremity of frost and penury, where a cave, a lock of straw, or a few leaves, is all their covering, and wild beasts their nourishment; all this by custom is not only made tolerable, but when it is once taken up upon necessity, by little and little, it becomes pleasant to them. Why should we then count that condition of life a calamity which is the lot of many nations? There is no state of life so miserable but that there are in it remissions, diversions, nay, and delights too; such is the benignity of Nature towards us, even in the severest accidents of human life. There were no living if adversity should hold on as it begins, and keep up the force of the first impression. We are apt to murmur at many things as great evils, that have nothing at all of evil in them besides the complaint, which we should more reasonably take up against ourselves. If I be sick, it is part of my fate; and for other calamities, they are usual things; they ought to be; nay, which is more, they must be, for they come by divine appointment. So that we should not only submit to God, but assent to him, and obey him out of *duty*, even if there were no *necessity*. All those terrible appearances that make us groan and tremble are but the tribute of life; we are neither to wish, nor to ask, nor to hope to escape them; for it is a kind of dishonesty to pay a tribute unwillingly. Am I troubled with the stone, or afflicted with continual losses? nay, is my body in danger? All this is no more than what I prayed for when I prayed for old age. All these things are as familiar in a long life, as dust and dirt in a long way. Life is a warfare; and what brave man would not rather choose to be in a tent than in shambles? Fortune does like a swordsman, she scorns to encounter a fearful man: there is no honor in the victory where there is no danger in the way to it; she tries Mucius by *fire*; Rutilius by *exile*; Socrates by *poison*; Cato by *death*.

It is only in adverse fortune, and in bad times, that we find great examples. Mucius thought himself happier with his hand in the flame, than if it had been in the bosom of his mistress. Fabricius took more pleasure in eating the roots of his own planting than in all the delicacies of luxury and expense. Shall we call Rutilius miserable, whom his very enemies have adored? who, upon a glorious and a public principle, chose rather to lose his country than to return from banishment? the only man that denied any thing to Sylla the dictator, who recalled him. Nor did he only refuse to come, but drew himself further off: "Let them," says he, "that think banishment a misfortune, live slaves at Rome, under the imperial cruelties of Sylla: he that sets a price upon the heads of senators; and after a law of his own institution against cut-throats, becomes the greatest himself." Is it not better for a man to live in exile abroad than to be massacred at home? In suffering for virtue, it is not the torment but the cause, that we are to consider; and the more pain, the more renown. When any hardship befalls us, we must look upon it as an act of Providence, which many times suffers particulars to be wounded for the conservation of the whole: beside that, God chastises some people under an appearance of blessing them, turning their prosperity to their ruin as a punishment for abusing his goodness. And we are further to consider, that many a good man is afflicted, only to teach others to suffer; for we are born for example; and likewise that where men are contumacious and refractory, it pleases God many times to cure greater evils by less, and to turn our miseries to our advantage.

How many casualties and difficulties are there that we dread as insupportable mischiefs, which, upon farther thoughts, we find to be mercies and benefits? as banishment, poverty, loss of relations, sickness, disgrace. Some are cured by the lance; by fire, hunger, thirst; taking out of bones, lopping off limbs, and the like: nor do we only fear things that are many times beneficial to us; but, on the other side, we hanker after and pursue things that are deadly and pernicious: we are poisoned in the very pleasure of our luxury, and betrayed to a thousand diseases by the indulging of our palate. To lose a child or a limb, is only to part with what we have received, and Nature may do what she pleases with her own. We are frail ourselves, and we have received things transitory – that which was given us may be taken away – calamity tries virtue as the fire does gold, nay, he that lives most at ease is only delayed, not dismissed, and his portion is to come. When we are visited with sickness or other afflictions we are not to murmur as if we were ill used – it is a mark of the general's esteem when he puts us upon a post of danger: we do not say "My captain uses me ill," but "he does me honor;" and so should we say that are commanded to encounter difficulties, for this is our case with God Almighty.

What was Regulus the worse, because Fortune made choice of him for an eminent instance both of faith and patience? He was thrown into a case of wood stuck with pointed nails, so that which way soever he turned his body, it rested upon his wounds; his eyelids were cut off to keep him waking; and yet Mecænas was not happier upon his *bed* than Regulus upon his *torments*. Nay, the world is not yet grown so wicked as not to prefer Regulus before Mecænas: and can any man take that to be an evil of which Providence accounted this brave man worthy? "It has pleased God," says he, "to single me out for an experiment of the force of human nature." No man knows his own strength or value but by being put to the proof. The pilot is tried in a storm; the soldier in a battle; the rich man knows not how to behave himself in poverty: he that has lived in popularity and applause, knows not how he would bear infamy and reproach: nor he that never had children how he would bear the loss of them. Calamity is the occasion of virtue, and a spur to a great mind. The very apprehension of a wound startles a man when he first bears arms; but an old soldier bleeds boldly, because he knows that a man may lose blood, and yet win the day. Nay, many times a calamity turns to our advantage; and great ruins have but made way to greater glories. The crying out of Fire! has many times quieted a fray, and the interposing of a wild beast has parted the thief and the traveller; for we are not at leisure for less mischiefs while we are under the apprehensions of greater. One man's life is saved by a disease: another is arrested, and taken out of the way, just when his house was falling upon his head.

To show now that the favors or the crosses of fortune, and the accidents of sickness and of health, are neither good nor evil, God permits them indifferently both to good and evil men. "It is hard," you will say, "for a virtuous man to suffer all sorts of misery, and for a wicked man not only to go free, but to enjoy himself at pleasure." And is it not the same thing for men of prostituted impudence and wickedness to sleep in a whole skin, when men of honor and honesty bear arms; lie in the trenches, and receive wounds? or for the vestal virgins to rise in the night to their prayers, when common strumpets lie stretching themselves in their beds? We should rather say with Demetrius, "If I had known the will of Heaven before I was called to it, I would have offered myself." If it be the pleasure of God to take my children, I have brought them up to that end: if my fortune, any part of my body, or my life, I would rather present it than yield it up: I am ready to part with all, and to suffer all; for I know that nothing comes to pass but what God appoints: our fate is decreed, and things do not so much happen, as in their due time proceed, and every man's portion of joy and sorrow is predetermined.

There is nothing falls amiss to a good man that can be charged upon Providence; for wicked actions, lewd thoughts, ambitious projects, blind lusts, and insatiable avarice – against all these he is armed by the benefit of reason: and do we expect now that God should look to our luggage too? (I mean our bodies.) Demetrius discharged himself of his treasure as the clog and burden of his mind: shall we wonder then if God suffers that to befall a good man which a good man sometimes does to himself? I lose a son, and why not, when it may sometimes so fall out that I myself may kill him? Suppose he be banished by an order of state, is it not the same thing with a man's voluntarily leaving his country never to return? Many afflictions may befall a good man, but no evil, for contraries will never incorporate – all the rivers in the world are never able to change the taste or quality of the sea. Prudence and religion are above accidents, and draw good out of every thing – affliction keeps a man in use, and makes him strong, patient, and hardy. Providence treats us like a generous father, and brings us up to labors, toils, and dangers; whereas the indulgence of a fond mother makes us weak and spiritless.

God loves us with a masculine love, and turns us loose to injuries and indignities: he takes delight to see a brave and a good man wrestling with evil fortune, and yet keeping himself upon his legs, when the whole world is in disorder about him. And are not we ourselves delighted, to see a bold fellow press with his lance upon a boar or lion? and the constancy and resolution of the action is the grace and dignity of the spectacle. No man can be happy that does not stand firm against all contingencies; and say to himself in all extremities, "I should have been content, if it might have been so or so, but since it is otherwise determined, God will provide better." The more we struggle with our necessities, we draw the knot the harder, and the worse it is with us: and the more a bird flaps and flutters in the snare, the surer she is caught: so that the best way is to submit and lie still, under this double consideration, that "the proceedings of God are unquestionable, and his decrees are not to be resisted."

CHAPTER IX.
OF LEVITY OF MIND, AND OTHER IMPEDIMENTS OF A HAPPY LIFE.

Now, to sum up what is already delivered, we have showed what happiness is, and wherein it consists: that it is founded upon wisdom and virtue; for we must first know what we ought to do, and then live according to that knowledge. We have also discoursed the helps of philosophy and precept toward a *happy life*; the blessing of a good conscience; that a good man can never be miserable, nor a wicked man happy; nor any man unfortunate that cheerfully submits to Providence. We shall now examine, how it comes to pass that, when the certain way to happiness lies so fair before us, men will yet steer their course on the other side, which as manifestly leads to ruin.

There are some that live without any design at all, and only pass in the world like straws upon a river; they do not go, but they are carried. Others only deliberate upon the parts of life, and not upon the whole, which is a great error: for there is no disposing of the circumstances of it, unless we first propound the main scope. How shall any man take his aim without a mark? or what wind will serve him that is not yet resolved upon his port? We live as it were by chance, and by chance we are governed. Some there are that torment themselves afresh with the memory of what is past: "Lord! what did I endure? never was any man in my condition; everybody gave me over; my very heart was ready to break," etc. Others, again, afflict themselves with the apprehension of evils to come; and very ridiculously: for the *one* does not *now* concern us, and the *other* not *yet*: beside that, there may be remedies for mischiefs likely to happen; for they give us warning by signs and symptoms of their approach. Let him that would be quiet take heed not to provoke men that are in power, but live without giving offence; and if we cannot make all great men our friends, it will suffice to keep them from being our enemies. This is a thing we must avoid, as a mariner would do a storm.

A rash seaman never considers what wind blows, or what course he steers, but runs at a venture, as if he would brave the rocks and the eddies; whereas he that is careful and considerate, informs himself beforehand where the danger lies, and what weather it is like to be: he consults his compass, and keeps aloof from those places that are infamous for wrecks and miscarriages; so does a wise man in the common business of life; he keeps out of the way from those that may do him hurt: but it is a point of prudence not to let them take notice that he does it on purpose; for that which a man shuns he tacitly condemns. Let him have a care also of *listeners, newsmongers,* and *meddlers* in other people's matters;

for their discourse is commonly of such things as are never profitable, and most commonly dangerous either to be spoken or heard.

Levity of mind is a great hindrance of repose, and the very change of wickedness is an addition to the wickedness itself; for it is inconstancy added to iniquity; we relinquish the thing we sought, and then we take it up again; and so divide our lives between our lust and our repentances. From one appetite we pass to another, not so much upon choice as for change; and there is a check of conscience that casts a damp upon all our unlawful pleasures, which makes us lose the day in expectation of the night, and the night itself for fear of the approaching light.

Some people are *never* at quiet, others are *always so*, and they are both to blame: for that which looks like vivacity and industry in the one is only a restlessness and agitation; and that which passes in the other for moderation and reserve is but a drowsy and unactive sloth. Let motion and rest both take their turns, according to the order of Nature, which makes both the day and the night. Some are perpetually shifting from one thing to another; others, again, make their whole life but a kind of uneasy sleep: some lie tossing and turning until very weariness brings them to rest; others, again, I cannot so properly call inconstant as lazy. There are many proprieties and diversities of vice; but it is one never-failing effect of it to live displeased.

We do all of us labor under inordinate desires; we are either timorous, and dare not venture, or venturing we do not succeed; or else we cast ourselves upon uncertain hopes, where we are perpetually solicitous, and in suspense. In this distraction we are apt to propose to ourselves things dishonest and hard; and when we have taken great pains to no purpose, we come then to repent of our undertakings: we are afraid to go on, and we can neither master our appetites nor obey them: we live and die restless and irresolute; and, which is worst of all, when we grow weary of the public, and betake ourselves to solitude for relief, our minds are sick and wallowing, and the very house and walls are troublesome to us; we grow impatient and ashamed of ourselves, and suppress our inward vexation until it breaks our heart for want of vent. This is it that makes us sour and morose, envious of others, and dissatisfied with ourselves; until at last, betwixt our troubles for other people's successes and the despair of our own, we fall foul upon Fortune and the times, and get into a corner perhaps, where we sit brooding over our own disquiets. In these dispositions there is a kind of pruriginous[2] fancy, that makes some people take delight in labor and uneasiness, like the clawing of an itch until the blood starts.

This is it that puts us upon rambling voyages; one while by land; but still disgusted with the present: the town pleases us to-day, the country to-morrow:

---

2. *Inflammatory eruption of the skin, hence itchy, lascivious*

the splendors of the court at one time, the horrors of a wilderness at another, but all this while we carry our plague about us; for it is not the place we are weary of, but ourselves. Nay, our weakness extends to everything; for we are impatient equally of toil and of pleasure. This trotting of the ring, and only treading the same steps over and over again, has made many a man lay violent hands upon himself. It must be the change of the mind, not of the climate, that will remove the heaviness of the heart; our vices go along with us, and we carry in ourselves the causes of our disquiets. There is a great weight lies upon us, and the bare shocking of it makes it the more uneasy; changing of countries, in this case, is not travelling, but wandering. We must keep on our course, if we would gain our journey's end. "He that cannot live happily anywhere, will live happily nowhere." What is a man the better for travelling? as if his cares could not find him out wherever he goes? Is there any retiring from the fear of death, or of torments? or from those difficulties which beset a man wherever he is? It is only philosophy that makes the mind invincible, and places us out of the reach of fortune, so that all her arrows fall short of us. This it is that reclaims the rage of our lusts, and sweetens the anxiety of our fears. Frequent changing of places or councils, shows an instability of mind; and we must fix the body before we can fix the soul. We can hardly stir abroad, or look about us, without encountering something or other that revives our appetites. As he that would cast off an unhappy love avoids whatsoever may put him in mind of the person, so he that would wholly deliver himself from his beloved lusts must shun all objects that may put them in his head again, and remind him of them. We travel, as children run up and down after strange sights, for novelty, not profit; we return neither the better nor the sounder; nay, and the very agitation hurts us. We learn to call towns and places by their names, and to tell stories of mountains and of rivers; but had not our time been better spent in the study of wisdom and of virtue? in the learning of what is already discovered, and in the quest of things not yet found out? If a man break his leg, or strain his ankle, he sends presently for a surgeon to set all right again, and does not take horse upon it, or put himself on ship-board; no more does the change of place work upon our disordered minds than upon our bodies. It is not the place, I hope, that makes either an orator or a physician. Will any man ask upon the road, Pray, which is the way to prudence, to justice, to temperance, to fortitude? No matter whither any man goes that carries his affections along with him. He that would make his travels delightful must make himself a temperate companion.

 A great traveller was complaining that he was never the better for his travels; "That is very true," said Socrates, "because you travelled with yourself." Now, had not he better have made himself another man than to transport himself to another place? It is no matter what manners we find anywhere; so long as we carry our own. But we have all of us a natural curiosity of seeing fine sights, and of making new discoveries, turning over antiquities, learning the customs of nations, etc. We are never quiet; to-day we seek an office, to-morrow we are sick of it. We divide our lives betwixt a dislike of the present and a desire of the future: but he that lives as he should, orders himself so, as neither to fear nor to wish for to-morrow; if it comes, it is welcome; but if not, there is nothing lost; for that which is come, is but the same over again with what is past. As levity is a pernicious enemy to quiet, so pertinacity is a great one too. The one changes nothing, the other sticks to nothing; and which of the two is the worse, may be a question. It is many times seen, that we beg earnestly for those things, which, if they were offered us, we would refuse; and it is but just to punish this easiness of asking with an equal facility of granting. There are some things we would be thought to desire, which we are so far from desiring that we dread them. "I shall tire you," says one, in the middle of a tedious story. "Nay, pray be pleased to go on," we cry, though we wish his tongue out at half-way: nay, we do not deal candidly even with God himself. We should say to ourselves in these cases, "This I have drawn upon myself. I could never be quiet until I had gotten this woman, this place, this estate, this honor, and now see what is come of it."

One sovereign remedy against all misfortunes is constancy of mind: the changing of parties and countenances looks as if a man were driven with the wind. Nothing can be above him that is above fortune. It is not violence, reproach, contempt, or whatever else from without, that can make a wise man quit his ground: but he is proof against calamities, both great and small: only our error is, that what we cannot do ourselves, we think nobody else can; so that we judge of the wise by the measures of the weak. Place me among princes or among beggars, the one shall not make me proud, nor the other ashamed. I can take as sound a sleep in a barn as in a palace, and a bundle of hay makes me as good a lodging as a bed of down. Should every day succeed to my wish, it should not transport me; nor would I think myself miserable if I should not have one quiet hour in my life. I will not transport myself with either pain or pleasure; but yet for all that, I could wish that I had an easier game to play, and that I were put rather to moderate my joys than my sorrows. If I were an imperial prince, I had rather take than be taken; and yet I would bear the same mind under the chariot of my conqueror that I had in my own. It is no great matter to trample upon those things that are most coveted or feared by the common people. There are those that will laugh upon the wheel, and cast themselves upon a certain death, only upon a transport of love, perhaps anger, avarice, or revenge; how much more then upon an instinct of virtue, which is invincible and steady! If a short obstinacy of mind can do this, how much more shall a composed and deliberate virtue, whose force is equal and perpetual.

To secure ourselves in this world, first, we must aim at nothing that men count worth the wrangling for. Secondly, we must not value the possession of any thing which even a common thief would think worth the stealing. A man's body is no booty. Let the way be never so dangerous for robberies, the poor and the naked pass quietly. A plain-dealing sincerity of manners makes a man's life happy, even in despite of scorn and contempt, which is every clear man's fate. But we had better yet be contemned for simplicity than lie perpetually upon the torture of a counterfeit; provided that care be taken not to confound simplicity with negligence; and it is, moreover, an uneasy life that of a disguise; for a man to seem to be what he is not, to keep a perpetual guard upon himself, and to live in fear of a discovery. He takes every man that looks upon him for a spy, over and above the trouble of being put to play another man's part. It is a good remedy in some cases for a man to apply himself to civil affairs and public business; and yet, in this state of life too, what betwixt ambition and calumny, it is hardly safe to be honest. There are, indeed, some cases wherein a wise man will give way; but let him not yield over easily neither; if he marches off, let him have a care of his honor, and make his retreat with his sword in his hand, and his face to the enemy. Of all others, a studious life is the least tiresome: it makes us easy to ourselves and to others, and gains us both friends and reputation.

CHAPTER X.
HE THAT SETS UP HIS REST UPON CONTINGENCIES SHALL NEVER BE QUIET.

Never pronounce any man happy that depends upon fortune for his happiness; for nothing can be more preposterous than to place the good of a reasonable creature in unreasonable things. If I have lost any thing, it was adventitious; and the less money, the less trouble; the less favor, the less envy; nay, even in those cases that put us out of their wits, it is not the loss itself, but the opinion of the loss, that troubles us. It is a common mistake to account those things necessary that are superfluous, and to depend upon fortune for the felicity of life, which arises only from virtue. There is no trusting to her smiles; the sea swells and rages in a moment, and the ships are swallowed at night, in the very place where they sported themselves in the morning. And fortune has the same power over princes that it has over empires, over nations that it has over cities, and the same power over cities that it has over private men. Where is that estate that may not be followed upon the heel with famine and beggary? that dignity which the next moment may not be laid in the dust? that kingdom that is secure from desolation and ruin? The period of all things is at hand, as well that which casts out the fortunate as the other that delivers the unhappy; and that which may fall out at any time may fall out this very day. What *shall* come to pass I know not, but what *may* come to pass I know: so that I will despair of nothing, but expect everything; and whatsoever Providence remits is clear gain. Every moment, if it spares me, deceives me; and yet in some sort it does not deceive me; for though I know that any thing may happen, yet I know likewise that everything will not. I will hope the best, and provide for the worst. Methinks we should not find so much fault with Fortune for her inconstancy when we ourselves suffer a change every moment that we live; only other changes make more noise, and this steals upon us like the shadow upon a dial, every jot as certainly, but more insensibly.

The burning of Lyons may serve to show us that we are never safe, and to arm us against all surprises. The terror of it must needs be great, for the calamity is almost without example. If it had been fired by an enemy, the flame would have left some further mischief to have been done by the soldiers; but to be wholly consumed, we have not heard of many earthquakes so pernicious: so many rarities to be destroyed in one night; and in the depth of peace to suffer an outrage beyond the extremity of war; who would believe it? but twelve hours betwixt so fair a city and none at all! It was laid in ashes in less time than it would require to tell the story.

To stand unshaken in such a calamity is hardly to be expected, and our wonder can but be equal to our grief. Let this accident teach us to provide against all possibilities that fall within the power of fortune. All external things are under her dominion: one while she calls our hands to her assistance; another while she contents herself with her own force, and destroys us with mischiefs of which we cannot find the author. No time, place, or condition, is excepted; she makes our very pleasures painful to us; she makes war upon us in the depth of peace, and turns the means of our security into an occasion of fear; she turns a friend into an enemy, and makes a foe of a companion; we suffer the effects of war without any adversary; and rather than fail, our felicity shall be the cause of our destruction. Lest we should either forget or neglect her power, every day produces something extraordinary. She persecutes the most temperate with sickness, the strongest constitutions with the phthisis[3]; she brings the innocent to punishment, and the most retired she assaults with tumults. Those glories that have grown up with many ages, with infinite labor and expense, and under the favor of many auspicious providences, one day scatters and brings to nothing. He that pronounced a day, nay, an hour, sufficient for the destruction of the greatest empire, might have fallen to a moment.

It were some comfort yet to the frailty of mankind and of human affairs, if things might but decay as slowly as they rise; but they grow by degrees, and they fall to ruin in an instant. There is no felicity in anything either private or public; men, nations, and cities, have all their fates and periods; our very entertainments are not without terror, and our calamity rises there where we least expect it. Those kingdoms that stood the shock both of foreign wars and civil, come to destruction without the sight of an enemy. Nay, we are to dread our peace and felicity more than violence, because we are here taken unprovided; unless in a state of peace we do the duty of men in war, and say to ourselves, *Whatsoever may be, will be*. I am to-day safe and happy in the love of my country; I am to-morrow banished: to-day in pleasure, peace, health; to-morrow broken upon a wheel, led in triumph, and in the agony of sickness. Let us therefore prepare for a shipwreck in the port, and for a tempest in a calm. One violence drives me from my country, another ravishes that from me; and that very place where a man can hardly pass this day for a crowd may be to-morrow a desert. Wherefore let us set before our eyes the whole condition of human nature, and consider as well what *may* happen as what commonly *does*. The way to make future calamities easy to us in the sufferance, is to make them familiar to us in the contemplation. How many cities in Asia, Achaia, Assyria, Macedonia, have been swallowed up by earthquakes? nay, whole countries are lost, and large provinces laid under water; but time brings all things to an end; for all the works of mortals are mortal; all possessions and their possessors are uncertain and perishable; and what wonder is it to lose anything at any time, when we must one day lose all?

---

3. *wasting disease; probably tuberculosis.*

That which we call our own is but lent us; and what we have received *gratis* we must return without complaint. That which Fortune gives us this hour she may take away the next; and he that trusts to her favors, shall either find himself deceived, or if he be not, he will at least be troubled, because he may be so. There is no defence in walls, fortifications, and engines, against the power of fortune; we must provide ourselves within, and when we are safe there, we are invincible; we may be battered, but not taken. She throws her gifts among us, and we sweat and scuffle for them, never considering how few are the better for that which is expected by all. Some are transported with what they get; others tormented for what they miss; and many times there is a leg or an arm broken in a contest for a counter. She gives us honors, riches, favors, only to take them away again, either by violence or treachery: so that they frequently turn to the damage of the receiver. She throws out baits for us, and sets traps as we do for birds and beasts; her bounties are snares and lime-twigs to us; we think that we take, but we are taken. If they had any thing in them that was substantial, they would some time or other fill and quiet us; but they serve only to provoke our appetite without anything more than pomp and show to allay it. But the best of it is, if a man cannot mend his fortune, he may yet mend his manners, and put himself so far out of her reach, that whether she gives or takes, it shall be all one to us; for we are neither the greater for the one, nor the less for the other. We call this a dark room, or that a light one; when it is in itself neither the one nor the other, but only as the day and the night render it. And so it is in riches, strength of body, beauty, honor, command: and likewise in pain, sickness, banishment, death: which are in themselves middle and indifferent things, and only good or bad as they are influenced by virtue. To weep, lament, and groan, is to renounce our duty; and it is the same weakness on the other side to exult and rejoice. I would rather make my fortune than expect it; being neither depressed with her injuries, nor dazzled with her favors. When Zeno was told, that all his goods were drowned; "Why then," says he, "Fortune has a mind to make me a philosopher." It is a great matter for a man to advance his mind above her threats or flatteries; for he that has once gotten the better of her is safe forever.

It is some comfort yet to the unfortunate, that great men lie under the lash for company; and that death spares the palace no more than the cottage, and that whoever is above me has a power also above him. Do we not daily see funerals without trouble, princes deposed, countries depopulated, towns sacked; without so much as thinking how soon it may be our own case? whereas, if we would but prepare and arm ourselves against the iniquities of fortune, we should never be surprised.

When we see any man banished, beggared, tortured, we are to account, that though the mischief fell upon another, it was levelled at us. What wonder is it if, of so many thousands of dangers that are constantly hovering about us, one comes to hit us at last? That which befalls any man, may befall every man; and then it breaks the force of a present calamity to provide against the future. Whatsoever our lot is, we must bear it: as suppose it be contumely, cruelty, fire, sword, pains, diseases, or a prey to wild beasts; there is no struggling, nor any remedy but moderation. It is to no purpose to bewail any part of our life, when life itself is miserable throughout; and the whole flux of it only a course of transition from one misfortune to another.

A man may as well wonder that he should be cold in winter, sick at sea, or have his bones clatter together in a wagon, as at the encounter of ill accidents and crosses in the passage of human life; and it is in vain to run away from fortune, as if there were any hiding-place wherein she could not find us; or to expect any quiet from her; for she makes life a perpetual state of war, without so much as any respite or truce. This we may conclude upon, that her empire is but imaginary, and that whosoever serves her, makes himself a voluntary slave; for "the things that are often contemned by the inconsiderate, and always by the wise, are in themselves neither good nor evil:" as pleasure and pains; prosperity and adversity; which can only operate upon our outward condition, without any proper and necessary effect upon the mind.

CHAPTER XI.
A SENSUAL LIFE IS A MISERABLE LIFE.

The sensuality that we here treat of falls naturally under the head of luxury; which extends to all the excesses of gluttony, lust, effeminacy of manners; and, in short, to whatsoever concerns the overgreat care of the carcass.

To begin now with the pleasures of the palate, (which deal with us like Egyptian thieves, that strangle those they embrace), what shall we say of the luxury of Nomentanus and Apicius, that entertained their very souls in the kitchen: they have the choicest music for their ears; the most diverting spectacles for their eyes; the choicest variety of meats and drinks for their palates. What is all this, I say, but a *merry madness*? It is true, they have their delights, but not without heavy and anxious thoughts, even in their very enjoyments, beside that, they are followed with repentance, and their frolics are little more than the laughter of so many people out of their wits. Their felicities are full of disquiet, and neither sincere nor well grounded: but they have need of one pleasure to support another; and of new prayers to forgive the errors of their former. Their life must needs be wretched that get with great pains what they keep with greater.

One diversion overtakes another; hope excites hope; ambition begets ambition; so that they only change the matter of their miseries, without seeking any end of them; and shall never be without either prosperous or unhappy causes of disquiet. What if a body might have all the pleasures in the world for the asking? who would so much unman himself, as by accepting of them, to desert his soul, and become a perpetual slave to his senses? Those false and miserable palates, that judge of meats by the price and difficulty, not by the healthfulness of taste, they vomit that they may eat, and they eat that they may fetch it up again. They cross the seas for rarities, and when they have swallowed them, they will not so much as give them time to digest. Wheresoever Nature has placed men, she has provided them aliment: but we rather choose to irritate hunger by expense than to allay it at an easier rate.

What is it that we plow the seas for; or arm ourselves against men and beasts? To what end do we toil, and labor, and pile bags upon bags? We may enlarge our fortunes, but we cannot our bodies; so that it does but spill and run over, whatsoever we take more than we can hold. Our forefathers (by the force of whose virtues we are now supported in our vices) lived every jot as well as we, when they provided and dressed their own meat with their own hands; lodged upon the ground, and were not as yet come to the vanity of gold and gems; when they swore by their earthen gods, and kept their oath, though they died for it.

Did not our consuls live more happily when they cooked their own meat with those victorious hands that had conquered so many enemies and won so many laurels? Did they not live more happily, I say, than our Apicius (that corrupter of youth, and plague of the age he lived in) who, after he had spent a prodigious fortune upon his belly, poisoned himself for fear of starving, when he had yet 250,000 crowns in his coffers? which may serve to show us, that it is the mind, and not the sum, that makes any man rich; when Apicius with all his treasure counted himself in a state of beggary, and took poison to avoid that condition, which another would have prayed for. But why do we call it poison, which was the wholesomest draught of his life? His daily gluttony was poison rather, both to himself and others. His ostentation of it was intolerable; and so was the infinite pains he took to mislead others by his example, who went even fast enough of themselves without driving.

It is a shame for a man to place his felicity in those entertainments and appetites that are stronger in brutes. Do not beasts eat with a better stomach? Have they not more satisfaction in their lusts? And they have not only a quicker relish of their pleasures, but they enjoy them without either scandal or remorse. If sensuality were happiness, beasts were happier than men; but human felicity is lodged in the soul, not in the flesh. They that deliver themselves up to luxury are still either tormented with too little, or oppressed with too much; and equally miserable, by being either deserted or overwhelmed: they are like men in a dangerous sea; one while cast a-dry upon a rock, and another while swallowed up in a whirlpool; and all this from the mistake of not distinguishing good from evil. The huntsman, that with much labor and hazard takes a wild beast, runs as great a risk afterwards in the keeping of him; for many times he tears out the throat of his master; and it is the same thing with inordinate pleasures: the more in number, and the greater they are, the more general and absolute a slave is the servant of them. Let the common people pronounce him as happy as they please, he pays his liberty for his delights, and sells himself for what he buys.

Let any man take a view of our kitchens, the number of our cooks, and the variety of our meats; will he not wonder to see so much provision made for one belly? We have as many diseases as we have cooks or meats; and the service of the appetite is the study now in vogue. To say nothing of our trains of lackeys, and our troops of caterers and sewers: Good God! that ever one belly should employ so many people! How nauseous and fulsome are the surfeits that follow these excesses? Simple meats are out of fashion, and all are collected into one; so that the cook does the office of the stomach; nay, and of the teeth too; for the meat looks as if it were chewed beforehand: here is the luxury of all tastes in one dish, and liker a vomit than a soup. From these compounded dishes arise compounded diseases, which require compounded medicines. It is the same thing with our minds that it is with our tables; simple vices are curable by simple counsels, but a general dissolution of manners is hardly overcome; we are overrun with a public as well as with a private madness. The physicians of old understood little more than the virtue of some herbs to stop blood, or heal a wound; and their firm and healthful bodies needed little more before they were corrupted by luxury and pleasure; and when it came to that once, their business was not to allay hunger, but to provoke it by a thousand inventions and sauces. That which was aliment to a craving stomach is become a burden to a full one. From hence came paleness, trembling, and worse effects from crudities than famine; a weakness in the joints, the belly stretched, suffusion of choler, the torpor of the nerves, and a palpitation of the heart. To say nothing of megrims, torments of the eyes and ears, head-ache, gout, scurvy, several sorts of fevers and putrid ulcers, with other diseases that are but the punishment of luxury. So long as our bodies were hardened with labor, or tired with exercise or hunting, our food was plain and simple; many dishes have made many diseases.

It is an ill thing for a man not to know the measure of his stomach, nor to consider that men do many things in their drink that they are ashamed of sober; drunkenness being nothing else but a voluntary madness. It emboldens men to do all sorts of mischiefs; it both irritates wickedness and discovers it; it does not make men vicious, but it shows them to be so. It was in a drunken fit that Alexander killed Clytus. It makes him that is insolent prouder, him that is cruel fiercer, it takes away all shame. He that is peevish breaks out presently into ill words and blows. The lecher, without any regard to decency or scandal, turns up his whore in the market-place. A man's tongue trips, his head runs round, he staggers in his pace. To say nothing of the crudities and diseases that follow upon this distemper, consider the public mischiefs it has done. How many warlike nations and strong cities, that have stood invincible to attacks and sieges, has drunkenness overcome! Is it not a great honor to drink the company dead? a magnificent virtue to swallow more wine than the rest, and yet at last to be outdone by a hogshead? What shall we say of those men that invert the offices of day and night? as if our eyes were only given us to make use of in the dark? Is it day? "It is time to go to bed." Is it night? "It is time to rise." Is it toward morning? "Let us go to supper." When other people lie down they rise, and lie till the next night to digest the debauch of the day before. It is an argument of clownery, to do as other people do.

Luxury steals upon us by degrees; first, it shows itself in a more than ordinary care of our bodies, it slips next into the furniture of our houses; and it gets then into the fabric, curiosity, and expense of the house itself. It appears, lastly, in the fantastical excesses of our tables. We change and shuffle our meats, confound our sauces, serve that in first that used to be last, and value our dishes, not for the taste, but for the rarity. Nay, we are so delicate, that we must be told when we are to eat or drink; when we are hungry or weary; and we cherish some vices as proofs and arguments of our happiness. The most miserable mortals are they that deliver themselves up to their palates, or to their lusts: the pleasure is short and turns presently nauseous, and the end of it is either shame or repentance. It is a brutal entertainment, and unworthy of a man, to place his felicity in the service of his senses. As to the wrathful, the contentious, the ambitious, though the distemper be great, the offence has yet something in it that is manly; but the basest of prostitutes are those that dedicate themselves wholly to lust; what with their hopes and fears, anxiety of thought, and perpetual disquiets, they are never well, full nor fasting.

What a deal of business is now made about our houses and diet, which was at first both obvious and of little expense? Luxury led the way, and we have employed our wits in the aid of our vices. First we desired superfluities, our next step was to wickedness, and, in conclusion, we delivered up our minds to our bodies, and so became slaves to our appetites, which before were our servants, and are now become our masters. What was it that brought us to the extravagance of embroideries, perfumes, tire-women, etc. We passed the bounds of Nature, and launched out into superfluities; insomuch, that it is now-a-days only for beggars and clowns to content themselves with what is sufficient; our luxury makes us insolent and mad. We take upon us like princes, and fly out for every trifle, as though there were life and death in the case. What a madness is it for a man to lay out an estate upon a table or a cabinet, a patrimony upon a pair of pendants, and to inflame the price of curiosities according to the hazard either of breaking or losing of them? To wear garments that will neither defend a woman's body, nor her modesty: so thin that one could make a conscience of swearing she were naked: for she hardly shows more in the privacies of her amour than in public? How long shall we covet and oppress, enlarge our possessions, and account that too little for one man which was formerly enough for a nation? And our luxury is as insatiable as our avarice. Where is that lake, that sea, that forest, that spot of land; that is not ransacked to gratify our palate? The very earth is burdened with our buildings; not a river, not a mountain, escapes us. Oh, that there should be such boundless desires in our little bodies! Would not fewer lodgings serve us? We lie but in one, and where we are not, that is not properly ours. What with our hooks, snares, nets, dogs, etc., we are at war with all living creatures; and nothing comes amiss but that which is either too cheap, or too common; and all this is to gratify a fantastical palate. Our avarice, our ambition, our lusts, are insatiable; we enlarge our possessions, swell our families, we rifle sea and land for matter of ornament and luxury. A bull contents himself with one meadow, and one forest is enough for a thousand elephants; but the little body of a man devours more than all other living creatures. We do not eat to satisfy hunger, but ambition; we are dead while we are alive, and our houses are so much our tombs, that a man might write our *epitaphs* upon our very doors.

A voluptuous person, in fine, can neither be a good man, a good patriot, nor a good friend; for he is transported with his appetites, without considering, that the law of Nature is the lot of man. A good man (like a good soldier) will stand his ground, receive wounds, glory in his scars, and in death itself love his master for whom he falls; with that divine precept always in his mind, "Follow good:" whereas he that complains, laments, and groans, must yield nevertheless, and do his duty though in spite of his heart. Now, what a madness is it for a man to choose rather to be lugged than to follow, and vainly to contend with the calamities of human life? Whatsoever is laid upon us by necessity, we should receive generously; for it is foolish to strive with what we cannot avoid. We are born subjects, and to obey God is perfect liberty. He that does this shall be free, safe, and quiet: all his actions shall succeed to his wish: and what can any man desire more than to want nothing from without, and to have all things desirable within himself? Pleasures do but weaken our minds, and send us for our support to Fortune, who gives us money only as the wages of slavery. We must stop our eyes and our ears. Ulysses had but one rock to fear, but human life has many. Every city, nay, every man, is one; and there is no trusting even to our nearest friends. Deliver me from the superstition of taking those things which are light and vain for felicities.

CHAPTER XII.
AVARICE AND AMBITION ARE INSATIABLE AND RESTLESS.

The man that would be truly rich must not increase his fortune, but retrench his appetites: for riches are not only superfluous, but mean, and little more to the possessor than to the looker-on. What is the end of ambition and avarice, when at best we are but stewards of what we falsely call our own? All those things that we pursue with so much hazard and expense of blood, as well to keep as to get, for which we break faith and friendship, what are they but the mere *deposita* of Fortune? and not ours, but already inclining toward a new master. There is nothing our own but that which we give to ourselves, and of which we have a certain and an inexpugnable possession. Avarice is so insatiable, that it is not in the power of liberality to content it; and our desires are so boundless, that whatever we get is but in the way to getting more without end: and so long as we are solicitous for the increase of wealth, we lose the true use of it; and spend our time in putting out, calling in, and passing our accounts, without any substantial benefit, either to the world or to ourselves. What is the difference betwixt old men and children? the one cries for nuts and apples, and the other for gold and silver: the one sets up courts of justice, hears and determines, acquits and condemns, in jest; the other in earnest: the one makes houses of clay, the other of marble: so that the works of old men are nothing in the world but the progress and improvement of children's errors; and they are to be admonished and punished too like children, not in revenge for injuries received, but as a correction of injuries done, and to make them give over. There is some substance yet in gold and silver; but as to judgments and statutes, procuration and continuance-money, these are only the visions and dreams of avarice.

Throw a crust of bread to a dog, he takes it open-mouthed, swallows it whole, and presently gapes for more: just so do we with the gifts of Fortune; down they go without chewing, and we are immediately ready for another chop. But what has avarice now to do with gold and silver, that is so much outdone by curiosities of a far greater value? Let us no longer complain that there was not a heavier load laid upon those precious metals, or that they were not buried deep enough, when we have found out ways by wax and parchments, and by bloody usurious contracts, to undo one another. It is remarkable, that Providence has given us all things for our advantage near at hand; but iron, gold, and silver, (being both the instrument of blood and slaughter, and the price of it) Nature has hidden in the bowels of the earth.

There is no avarice without some punishment, over and above that which it is to itself. How miserable is it in the desire! how miserable even in the attaining of our ends! For money is a greater torment in the possession than it is in the pursuit. The fear of losing it is a great trouble, the loss of it a greater, and it is made a greater yet by opinion. Nay, even in the case of no direct loss at all, the covetous man loses what he does not get. It is true, the people call the rich man a happy man, and wish themselves in his condition; but can any condition be worse than that which carries vexation and envy along with it? Neither is any man to boast of his fortune, his herds of cattle, his number of slaves, his lands and palaces; for comparing that which he has to that which he further covets, he is a beggar. No man can possess all things, but any man may contemn them; and the contempt of riches is the nearest way to the gaining of them.

Some magistrates are made for money, and those commonly are bribed with money. We are all turned merchants, and look not into the quality of things, but into the price of them; for reward we are pious, and for reward again we are impious. We are honest so long as we may thrive upon it; but if the devil himself gives better wages, we change our party. Our parents have trained us up into an admiration of gold and silver, and the love of it is grown up with us to that degree that when we would show our gratitude to Heaven, we make presents of those metals. This it is that makes poverty look like a curse and a reproach; and the poets help it forward; the chariot of the sun must be all of gold; the best of times must be the Golden Age, and thus they turn the greatest misery of mankind into the greatest blessings.

Neither does avarice make us only unhappy in ourselves, but malevolent also to mankind. The soldier wishes for war; the husbandman would have his corn dear; the lawyer prays for dissension; the physician for a sickly year; he that deals in curiosities, for luxury and excess, for he makes up his fortunes out of the corruptions of the age. High winds and public conflagrations make work for the carpenter and bricklayer, and one man lives by the loss of another; some few, perhaps, have the fortune to be detected, but they are all wicked alike. A great plague makes work for the sexton; and, in one word, whosoever gains by the dead has not much kindness for the living. Demades of Athens condemned a fellow that sold necessaries for funerals, upon proof that he wished to make himself a fortune by his trade, which could not be but by a great mortality; but perhaps he did not so much desire to have many customers, as to sell dear, and buy cheap; besides, that all of that trade might have been condemned as well as he. Whatsoever whets our appetites, flatters and depresses the mind, and, by dilating it, weakens it; first blowing it up, and then filling and deluding it with vanity.

To proceed now from the most prostitute of all vices, sensuality and avarice, to that which passes in the world for the most generous, the thirst of glory and dominion. If they that run mad after wealth and honor, could but look into the hearts of them that have already gained these points, how would it startle them to see those hideous cares and crimes that wait upon ambitious greatness: all those acquisitions that dazzle the eyes of the vulgar are but false pleasures, slippery and uncertain. They are achieved with labor, and the very guard of them is painful. Ambition puffs us up with vanity and wind: and we are equally troubled either to see any body before us, or nobody behind us; so that we lie under a double envy; for whosoever envies another is also envied himself. What matters it how far Alexander extended his conquests, if he was not yet satisfied with what he had? Every man wants as much as he covets; and it is lost labor to pour into a vessel that will never be full. He that had subdued so many princes and nations, upon the killing of Clytus (one friend) and the loss of Hyphestion (another) delivered himself up to anger and sadness; and when he was master of the world, he was yet a slave to his passions. Look into Cyrus, Cambyses, and the whole Persian line, and you shall not find so much as one man of them that died satisfied with what he had gotten. Ambition aspires from great things to greater; and propounds matters even impossible, when it has once arrived at things beyond expectation. It is a kind of dropsy; the more a man drinks, the more he covets. Let any man but observe the tumults and the crowds that attend palaces; what affronts must we endure to be admitted, and how much greater when we are in! The passage to virtue is fair, but the way to greatness is craggy and it stands not only upon a precipice, but upon ice too; and yet it is a hard matter to convince a great man that his station is slippery, or to prevail with him not to depend upon his greatness; but all superfluities are hurtful. A rank crop lays the corn; too great a burden of fruit breaks the bough; and our minds may be as well overcharged with an immoderate happiness. Nay, though we ourselves would be at rest, our fortune will not suffer it: the way that leads to honor and riches leads to troubles; and we find the source of our sorrows in the very objects of our delights.

What joy is there in feasting and luxury; in ambition and a crowd of clients; in the arms of a mistress, or in the vanity of an unprofitable knowledge? These short and false pleasures deceive us, and, like drunkenness, revenge the jolly madness of *one* hour with the nauseous and sad repentance of *many*. Ambition is like a gulf: everything is swallowed up in it and buried, beside the dangerous consequences of it; for that which one has taken from all, may be easily taken away again by all from one. It was not either virtue or reason, but the mad love of a deceitful greatness, that animated Pompey in his wars, either abroad or at home. What was it but his ambition that hurried him to Spain, Africa, and elsewhere, when he was too great already in everybody's opinion but his own? And the same motive had Julius Cæsar, who could not, even then, brook a superior himself, when the commonwealth had submitted unto two already.

Nor was it any instinct of virtue that pushed on Marius, who at the head of an army was himself led on under the command of ambition: but he came at last to the deserved fate of other wicked men, and to drink himself of the same cup that he had filled to others. We impose upon our reason, when we suffer ourselves to be transported with titles; for we know that they are nothing but a more glorious sound; and so for ornaments and gildings, though there be a lustre to dazzle our eyes, our understanding tells us that it is only outside, and the matter under it is only coarse and common.

I will never envy those that the people call great and happy. A sound mind is not to be shaken with a popular and vain applause; nor is it in the power of their pride to disturb the state of our happiness. An honest man is known now-a-days by the dust he raises upon the way, and it is become a point of honor to overrun people, and keep all at a distance; though he that is put out of the way may perchance be happier than he that takes it. He that would exercise a power profitable to himself, and grievous to nobody else, let him practice it upon his passion. They that have burnt cities, otherwise invincible, driven armies before them, and bathed themselves in human blood, after they have overcome all open enemies, they have been vanquished by their lust, by their cruelty, and without any resistance.

Alexander was possessed with the madness of laying kingdoms waste. He began with Greece, where he was brought up; and there he quarried himself upon that in it which was the best; he enslaved Lacedemon, and silenced Athens: nor was he content with the destruction of those towns which his father Philip had either conquered or bought; but he made himself the enemy of human nature; and, like the worst of beasts, he worried what he could not eat.

Felicity is an unquiet thing; it torments itself, and puzzles the brain. It makes some people ambitious, others luxurious; it puffs up some, and softens others; only (as it is with wine) some heads bear it better than others; but it dissolves all. Greatness stands upon a precipice: and if prosperity carries a man never so little beyond his poise, it overbears and dashes him to pieces. It is a rare thing for a man in a great fortune to lay down his happiness gently; it being a common fate for a man to sink under the weight of those felicities that raise him. How many of the nobility did Marius bring down to herdsmen and other mean offices! Nay, in the very moment of our despising servants, we may be made so ourselves.

CHAPTER XIII.
HOPE AND FEAR ARE THE BANE OF HUMAN LIFE.

No man can be said to be perfectly happy that runs the risk of disappointment: which is the case of every man that *fears* or *hopes* for anything. For *hope* and *fear*, how distant soever they may seem to be the one from the other, they are both of them yet coupled in the same chain, as the guard and the prisoner; and the one treads upon the heels of the other. The reason of this is obvious, for they are passions that look forward, and are ever solicitous for the future; only hope is the more plausible weakness of the two, which in truth, upon the main, are inseparable; for the one cannot be without the other: but where the hope is stronger than the fear, or the fear than the hope, we call it the one or the other; for without fear it were no longer hope, but *certainty*; as without hope it were no longer fear but *despair*.

We may come to understand whether our disputes are vain or not, if we do but consider that we are either troubled about the *present*, the *future* or *both*. If the present, it is easy to judge, and the future is uncertain. It is a foolish thing to be miserable beforehand for fear of misery to come; for a man loses the present, which he might enjoy, in expectation of the future: nay, the fear of losing anything is as bad as the loss itself. I will be as prudent as I can, but not timorous or careless; and I will bethink myself, and forecast what inconveniences may happen before they come. It is true, a man may fear, and yet not be fearful; which is no more than to have the affection of fear without the vice of it; but yet a frequent admittance of it runs into a habit. It is a shameful and an unmanly thing to be doubtful, timorous, and uncertain; to set one step forward, and another backward; and to be irresolute. Can there be any man so fearful, that had not rather fall once than hang always in suspense?

Our miseries are endless, if we stand in fear of all possibilities; the best way, in such a case, is to drive out one nail with another, and a little to qualify fear with hope; which may serve to palliate a misfortune; though not to cure it. There is not anything that we fear, which is so certain to come, as it is certain that many things which we do fear will not come; but we are loth to oppose our credulity when it begins to move us, and so to bring our fear to the test.

Well! but "what if the thing we fear should come to pass?" Perhaps it will be the better for us. Suppose it be *death* itself, why may it not prove the glory of my life? Did not poison make Socrates famous? and was not Cato's sword a great part of his honor?

"Do we fear any misfortune to befall us?" We are not presently sure that it will happen. How many deliverances have come unlooked for? and how many mischiefs that we looked for have never come to pass? It is time enough to lament when it comes, and, in the *interim*, to promise ourselves the best. What do I know but something or other may delay or divert it? Some have escaped out of the fire; others, when a house has fallen over their head, have received no hurt: one man has been saved when a sword was at his throat; another has been condemned, and outlived his headsman: so that ill-fortune, we see, as well as good, has her levities; peradventure it will be, peradventure not; and until it comes to pass, we are not sure of it: we do many times take words in a worse sense than they were intended, and imagine things to be worse taken than they are. It is time enough to bear a misfortune when it comes, without anticipating it.

He that would deliver himself from all apprehensions of the future, let him first take for granted, that all fears will fall upon him; and then examine and measure the evil that he fears, which he will find to be neither great nor long. Beside, that the ills which he fears he may suffer, he suffers in the very fear of them. As in the symptoms of an approaching disease, a man shall find himself lazy and listless: a weariness in his limbs, with a yawning and shuddering all over him; so it is in the case of a weak mind, it fancies misfortunes, and makes a man wretched before his time. Why should I torment myself at present with what, perhaps, may fall out fifty years hence? This humor is a kind of voluntary disease, and an industrious contrivance of our own unhappiness, to complain of an affliction that we do not feel. Some are not only moved with grief itself, but with the mere opinion of it; as children will start at a shadow, or at the sight of a deformed person. If we stand in fear of violence from a powerful enemy, it is some comfort to us, that whosoever makes himself terrible to others is not without fear himself: the least noise makes a lion start; and the fiercest of beasts, whatsoever enrages them, makes them tremble too: a shadow, a voice, an unusual odor, rouses them.

The things most to be feared I take to be of three kinds; *want, sickness*, and those *violences* that may be imposed upon us by a *strong hand*. The last of these has the greatest force, because it comes attended with noise and tumult; whereas the incommodities of poverty and diseases are more natural, and steal upon us in silence, without any external circumstances of horror: but the other marches in pomp, with fire and sword, gibbets, racks, hooks; wild beasts to devour us; stakes to impale us; engines to tear us to pieces; pitched bags to burn us in, and a thousand other exquisite inventions of cruelty. No wonder then, if that be the most dreadful to us that presents itself in so many uncouth shapes; and by the very solemnity is rendered the most formidable. The more instruments of bodily pain the executioner shows us, the more frightful he makes himself: for many a man that would have encountered death in any generous form, with resolution enough, is yet overcome with the *manner* of it.

As for the calamities of hunger and thirst, inward ulcers, scorching fevers, tormenting fits of the stone, I look upon these miseries to be at least as grievous as any of the rest; only they do not so much affect the fancy, because they lie out of sight. Some people talk high of danger at a distance; but (like cowards) when the executioner comes to do his duty, and show us the fire, the ax, the scaffold, and death at hand, their courage fails them upon the very pinch, when they have most need of it. Sickness, (I hope) captivity, fire, are no new things to us; the fall of houses, funerals, and conflagrations, are every day before our eyes. The man that I supped with last night is dead before morning; why should I wonder then, seeing so many fall about me, to be hit at last myself? What can be greater madness than to cry out, "Who would have dreamed of this?" And why not, I beseech you? Where is that estate that may not be reduced to beggary? that dignity which may not be followed with banishment, disgrace, and extreme contempt? that kingdom that may not suddenly fall to ruin; change its master, and be depopulated? that prince that may not pass the hand of a common hangman? That which is one man's fortune may be another's; but the foresight of calamities to come breaks the violence of them.

CHAPTER XIV.
IT IS ACCORDING TO THE TRUE OR FALSE ESTIMATE OF THINGS THAT WE ARE HAPPY OR MISERABLE.

How many things are there that the fancy makes terrible by night, which the day turns into ridiculous! What is there in labor, or in death, that a man should be afraid of? They are much slighter in act than in contemplation; and we *may* contemn them, but we *will* not: so that it is not because they are hard that we dread them, but they are hard because we are first afraid of them. Pains, and other violences of Fortune, are the same thing to us that goblins are to children: we are more scared with them than hurt. We take up our opinions upon trust, and err for company, still judging that to be best that has most competitors. We make a false calculation of matters, because we advise with opinion, and not with Nature; and this misleads us to a higher esteem for riches, honor, and power, than they are worth: we have been used to admire and recommend them, and a private error is quickly turned into a public. The greatest and the smallest things are equally hard to be comprehended; we account many things *great*, for want of understanding what effectually is so: and we reckon other things to be *small*, which we find frequently to be of the highest value. Vain things only move vain minds. The accidents that we so much boggle at are not terrible in themselves, but they are made so by our infirmities; but we consult rather what we hear than what we feel, without examining, opposing, or discussing the things we fear; so that we either stand still and tremble, or else directly run for it, as those troops did, that, upon the raising of the dust, took a flock of sheep for the enemy. When the body and mind are corrupted, it is no wonder if all things prove intolerable; and not because they are so in truth, but because we are dissolute and foolish: for we are infatuated to such a degree, that, betwixt the common madness of men, and that which falls under the care of the physician, there is but this difference, the one labors of a disease, and the other of a false opinion.

The Stoics hold, that all those torments that commonly draw from us groans and ejaculations, are in themselves trivial and contemptible. But these high-flown expressions apart (how true soever) let us discourse the point at the rate of ordinary men, and not make ourselves miserable before our time; for the things we apprehend to be at hand may possibly never come to pass. Some things trouble us more than they should, other things sooner; and some things again disorder us that ought not to trouble us at all; so that we either enlarge, or create, or anticipate our disquiets. For the first part, let it rest as a matter in controversy; for that which I account light, another perhaps will judge insupportable! One man laughs under the lash, and another whines for a fillip. How sad a calamity is poverty to one man, which to another appears rather desirable than inconvenient? For the poor man, who has nothing to lose, has nothing to fear: and he that would enjoy himself to the satisfaction of his soul, must be either poor indeed, or at least look as if he were so. Some people are extremely dejected with sickness and pain; whereas Epicurus blessed his fate with his last breath, in the acutest torments of the stone imaginable. And so for banishment, which to one man is so grievous, and yet to another is no more than a bare change of place: a thing that we do every day for our health, pleasure, nay, and upon the account even of common business.

How terrible is death to one man, which to another appears the greatest providence in nature, even toward all ages and conditions! It is the wish of some, the relief of many, and the end of all. It sets the slave at liberty, carries the banished man home, and places all mortals upon the same level: insomuch, that life itself were a punishment without it. When I see tyrants, tortures, violences, the prospect of death is a consolation to me, and the only remedy against the injuries of life.

Nay, so great are our mistakes in the true estimate of things, that we have hardly done any thing that we have not had reason to wish undone; and we have found the things we feared to be more desirable than those we coveted. Our very prayers have been more pernicious than the curses of our enemies; and we must pray to have our former prayers forgiven. Where is the wise man that wishes to himself the wishes of his mother, nurse, or his tutor; the worst of enemies, with the intention of the best of friends. We are undone if their prayers be heard; and it is our duty to pray that they may not; for they are no other than well-meaning execrations. They take evil for good, and one wish fights with another: give me rather the contempt of all those things whereof they wish me the greatest plenty. We are equally hurt by some that pray for us, and by others that curse us: the one imprints in us a false fear, and the other does us mischief by a mistake: so that it is no wonder if mankind be miserable, when we are brought up from the very cradle under the imprecations of our parents. We pray for trifles, without so much as thinking of the greatest blessings; and we are not ashamed many times to ask God for that which we should blush to own to our neighbor.

It is with us as with an innocent that my father had in his family; she fell blind on a sudden, and nobody could persuade her she was blind. "She could not endure the house," she cried, "it was so dark," and was still calling to go abroad. That which we laughed at in her we find to be true in ourselves, we are covetous and ambitious; but the world shall never bring us to acknowledge it, and we impute it to the place: nay, we are the worse of the two; for that blind fool called for a guide, and we wander about without one. It is a hard matter to cure those that will not believe they are sick. We are ashamed to admit a master, and we are too old to learn.

Vice still goes before virtue: so that we have two works to do: we must cast off the one, and learn the other. By one evil we make way to another, and only seek things to be avoided, or those of which we are soon weary. That which seemed too much when we wished for it, proves too little when we have it; and it is not, as some imagine, that felicity is greedy, but it is little and narrow, and cannot satisfy us. That which we take to be very high at a distance, we find to be but low when we come at it. And the business is, we do not understand the true state of things: we are deceived by rumors; when we have gained the thing we aimed at, we find it to be either ill or empty; or perchance less than we expect, or otherwise perhaps great, but not good.

CHAPTER XV.
THE BLESSINGS OF TEMPERANCE AND MODERATION.

There is not anything that is necessary to us but we have it either *cheap* or *gratis*: and this is the provision that our heavenly Father has made for us, whose bounty was never wanting to our needs. It is true the belly craves and calls upon us, but then a small matter contents it: a little bread and water is sufficient, and all the rest is but superfluous. He that lives according to reason shall never be poor, and he that governs his life by opinion shall never be rich: for nature is limited, but fancy is boundless. As for meat, clothes, and lodging, a little feeds the body, and as little covers it; so that if mankind would only attend human nature, without gaping at superfluities, a cook would be found as needless as a soldier: for we may have necessaries upon very easy terms; whereas we put ourselves to great pains for excesses. When we are cold, we may cover ourselves with skins of beasts; and, against violent heats, we have natural grottoes; or with a few osiers and a little clay we may defend ourselves against all seasons. Providence has been kinder to us than to leave us to live by our wits, and to stand in need of invention and arts.

It is only pride and curiosity that involve us in difficulties: if nothing will serve a man but rich clothes and furniture, statues and plate, a numerous train of servants, and the rarities of all nations, it is not Fortune's fault, but his own, that he is not satisfied: for his desires are insatiable, and this is not a thirst, but a disease; and if he were master of the whole world, he would be still a beggar. It is the mind that makes us rich and happy, in what condition soever we are; and money signifies no more to it than it does to the gods. If the religion be sincere, no matter for the ornaments it is only luxury and avarice that make poverty grievous to us; for it is a very small matter that does our business; and when we have provided against cold, hunger, and thirst, all the rest is but vanity and excess: and there is no need of expense upon foreign delicacies, or the artifices of the kitchen. What is he the worse for poverty that despises these things? nay, is he not rather the better for it, because he is not able to go to the price of them? for he is kept sound whether he will or not: and that which a man *cannot* do, looks many times as if he *would not*.

When I look back into the moderation of past ages, it makes me ashamed to discourse, as if poverty had need of any consolation; for we are now come to that degree of intemperance, that a fair patrimony is too little for a meal. Homer had but one servant, Plato three, and Zeno (the master of the masculine sect of Stoics) had none at all. The daughters of Scipio had their portions out of the common treasury, for their father left them not a penny: how happy were the husbands that had the people of Rome for their father-in-law! Shall any man now contemn poverty after these eminent examples, which are sufficient not only to justify but to recommend it? Upon Diogenes' only servant running away from him, he was told where he was, and persuaded to fetch him back again: "What," says he, "can Manes live without Diogenes, and not Diogenes without Manes?" and so let him go.

The piety and moderation of Scipio have made his memory more venerable than his arms; and more yet after he left his country than while he defended it: for matters were come to that pass, that either Scipio must be injurious to Rome or Rome to Scipio. Coarse bread and water to a temperate man is as good as a feast; and the very herbs of the field yield a nourishment to man as well as to beasts. It was not by choice meats and perfumes that our forefathers recommended themselves, but in virtuous actions, and the sweat of honest, military, and of manly labors.

While Nature lay in common, and all her benefits were promiscuously enjoyed, what could be happier than the state of mankind, when people lived without avarice or envy? What could be richer than when there was not a poor man to be found in the world? So soon as this impartial bounty of Providence came to be restrained by covetousness, and that particulars appropriated to themselves that which was intended for all, then did poverty creep into the world, when some men, by desiring more than came to their share, lost their title to the rest; a loss never to be repaired; for though we may come yet to get much, we once had all. The fruits of the earth were in those days divided among the inhabitants of it, without either want or excess. So long as men contented themselves with their lot, there was no violence, no engrossing or hiding of those benefits for particular advantages, which were appointed for the community; but every man had as much care for his neighbor as for himself. No arms or bloodshed, no war, but with wild beasts: but under the protection of a wood or a cave, they spent their days without cares, and their nights without groans; their innocence was their security and their protection. There were as yet no beds of state, no ornaments, of pearl or embroidery, nor any of those remorses that attend them; but the heavens were their canopy, and the glories of them their spectacle. The motions of the orbs, the courses of the stars, and the wonderful order of Providence, was their contemplation. There was no fear of the house falling, or the rustling of a rat behind the arras; they had no palaces then like cities; but they had open air, and breathing room, crystal fountains, refreshing shades, the meadows dressed up in their native beauty, and such cottages as were according to nature, and wherein they lived contentedly, without fear either of losing or of falling. These people lived without either solitude or fraud; and yet I must call them rather happy than wise.

That men were generally better before they were corrupted than after, I make no doubt; and I am apt to believe that they were both stronger and hardier too but their wits were not yet come to maturity; for Nature does not give virtue; and it is a kind of art to become good. They had not as yet torn up the bowels of the earth for gold, silver, or precious stones; and so far were they from killing any man, as we do, for a spectacle, that they were not as yet come to it, either in fear or anger; nay, they spared the very fishes. But, after all this, they were innocent because they were ignorant: and there is a great difference betwixt not knowing how to offend and not being willing to do it. They had, in that rude life, certain images and resemblances of virtue, but yet they fell short of virtue itself, which comes only by institution, learning, and study, as it is perfected by practice. It is indeed the end for which we were born, but yet it did not come into the world with us; and in the best of men, before they are instructed, we find rather the matter and the seeds of virtue than the virtue itself. It is the wonderful benignity of Nature that has laid open to us all things that may do us good, and only hid those things from us that may hurt us; as if she durst not trust us with gold and silver, or with iron, which is the instrument of war and contention, for the other. It is we ourselves that have drawn out of the earth both the *causes* and the *instruments* of our dangers: and we are so vain as to set the highest esteem upon those things to which Nature has assigned the lowest place. What can be more coarse and rude in the mine than these precious metals, or more slavish and dirty than the people that dig and work them? and yet they defile our minds more than our bodies, and make the possessor fouler than the artificer of them. Rich men, in fine, are only the greater slaves; both the one and the other want a great deal.

Happy is that man that eats only for hunger, and drinks only for thirst; that stands upon his own legs, and lives by reason, not by example; and provides for use and necessity, not for ostentation and pomp! Let us curb our appetites, encourage virtue, and rather be beholden to ourselves for riches than to Fortune, who when a man draws himself into a narrow compass, has the least mark at him. Let my bed be plain and clean, and my clothes so too: my meat without much expense, or many waiters, and neither a burden to my purse nor to my body, not to go out the same way it came in. That which is too little for luxury, is abundantly enough for nature. The end of eating and drinking is satiety; now, what matters it though one eats and drinks more, and another less, so long as the one is not a-hungry, nor the other athirst? Epicurus, who limits pleasure to nature, as the Stoics do virtue, is undoubtedly in the right; and those that cite him to authorize their voluptuousness do exceedingly mistake him, and only seek a good authority for an evil cause: for their pleasures of sloth, gluttony, and lust, have no affinity at all with his precepts or meaning. It is true, that at first sight his philosophy seems effeminate; but he that looks nearer him will find him to be a very brave man only in a womanish dress.

It is a common objection, I know, that these philosophers do not live at the rate they talk; for they can flatter their superiors, gather estates, and be as much concerned at the loss of fortune, or of friends, as other people: as sensible of reproaches, as luxurious in their eating and drinking, their furniture, their houses;

as magnificent in their plate, servants, and officers; as profuse and curious in their gardens, etc. Well! and what of all this, or if it were twenty times more? It is some degree of virtue for a man to condemn himself; and if he cannot come up to the best, to be yet better than the worst; and if he cannot wholly subdue his appetites, however to check and diminish them. If I do not live as I preach, take notice that I do not speak of myself, but of virtue, nor am I so much offended with other men's vices as with my own.

All this was objected to Plato, Epicurus, Zeno; nor is any virtue so sacred as to escape malevolence. The Cynic Demetrius was a great instance of severity and mortification; and one that imposed upon himself neither to possess anything, nor so much as to ask it: and yet he had this *scorn* put upon him, that his profession was *poverty*, not *virtue*. Plato is blamed for *asking* money; Aristotle for *receiving* it; Democritus for *neglecting* it; Epicurus for *consuming* it. How happy were we if we could but come to imitate these men's vices; for if we knew our own condition, we should find work enough at home. But we are like people that are making merry at a play or a tavern when their own houses are on fire, and yet they know nothing of it. Nay, Cato himself was said to be a drunkard; but *drunkenness* itself shall sooner be proved to be no crime than Cato dishonest. They that demolish temples, and overturn altars, show their good-will, though they can do the gods no hurt, and so it fares with those that invade the reputation of great men.

If the professors of virtue be as the world calls them, avaricious, libidinous, ambitious – what are they then that have a detestation for the very name of it: but malicious natures do not want wit to abuse honester men than themselves. It is the practice of the multitude to bark at eminent men as little dogs do at strangers; for they look upon other men's virtues as the upbraiding of their own wickedness. We should do well to commend those that are good, if not, let us pass them over; but, however, let us spare ourselves: for beside the blaspheming of virtue, our rage is to no purpose. But to return now to my text.

We are ready enough to limit others but loth to put bonds and restraints upon ourselves, though we know that many times a greater evil is cured by a less; and the mind that will not be brought to virtue by precepts, comes to it frequently by necessity. Let us try a little to eat upon a joint stool, to serve ourselves, to live within compass, and accommodate our clothes to the end they were made for. Occasional experiments of our moderation give us the best proof of our firmness and virtue. A well-governed appetite is a great part of liberty, and it is a blessed lot, that since no man can have all things that he would have, we may all of us forbear desiring what we have not. It is the office of temperance to overrule us in our pleasures; some she rejects, others she qualifies and keeps within bounds. Oh! the delights of rest when a man comes to be weary, and of meat when he is heartily hungry.

I have learned (says our author) by one journey how many things we have that are superfluous, and how easily they might be spared, for when we are without them upon necessity, we do not so much as feel the want of them. This is the second blessed day (says he) that my friend and I have travelled together: one wagon carries ourselves and our servants; my mattress lies upon the ground and I upon that: our diet answerable to our lodging, and never without our figs and our table-books. The muleteer without shoes, and the mules only prove themselves to be alive by their walking. In this equipage, I am not willing, I perceive, to own myself, but as often as we happen into better company, I presently fall a-blushing, which shows that I am not yet confirmed in those things which I approve and commend. I am not yet come to own my frugality, for he that is ashamed to be seen in a mean condition would be proud of a splendid one. I value myself upon what passengers think of me, and tacitly renounce my principles, whereas I should rather lift up my voice to be heard by mankind, and tell them "You are all mad – your minds are set upon superfluities and you value no man for his virtues."

I came one night weary home, and threw myself upon the bed with this consideration about me: "There is nothing ill that is well taken." My baker tells me he has no bread; but, says he, I may get some of your tenants, though I fear it is not good. No matter, said I, for I will stay until it be better – that is to say until my stomach will be glad of worse. It is discretion sometimes to practice temperance and wont ourselves to a little, for there are many difficulties both of time and place that may force us upon it.

When we come to the matter of patrimony, how strictly do we examine what every man is worth before we will trust him with a penny! "Such a man," we cry, "has a great estate, but it is shrewdly encumbered – a very fair house, but it was built with borrowed money – a numerous family, but he does not keep touch with his creditors – if his debts were paid he would not be worth a groat." Why do we not take the same course in other things, and examine what every man is worth? It is not enough to have a long train of attendants, vast possessions, or an incredible treasure in money and jewels – a man may be poor for all this. There is only this difference at best – one man borrows of the *usurer*, and the other of *fortune*. What signifies the carving or gilding of the chariot; is the master ever the better of it?

We cannot close up this chapter with a more generous instance of moderation than that of Fabricius. Pyrrhus tempted him with a sum of money to betray his country, and Pyrrhus's physician offered Fabricius, for a sum of money, to poison his *master*; but he was too brave either to be overcome by gold, or to be overcome by poison, so that he refused the money, and advised Pyrrhus to have a care of treachery: and this too in the heat of a licentious war. Fabricius valued himself upon his poverty, and was as much above the thought of riches as of poison. "Live Pyrrhus," says he "by my friendship; and turn that to thy satisfaction which was before thy trouble:" that is to say that Fabricius could not be corrupted.

CHAPTER XVI.

CONSTANCY OF MIND GIVES A MAN REPUTATION, AND MAKES HIM HAPPY IN DESPITE OF ALL MISFORTUNE.

The whole duty of man may be reduced to the two points of *abstinence* and *patience*; *temperance* in *prosperity*, and *courage* in *adversity*. We have already treated of the former: and the other follows now in course.

Epicurus will have it, that a wise man will *bear all injuries*; but the Stoics will not allow those things to be *injuries* which Epicurus calls so. Now, betwixt these two, there is the same difference that we find betwixt two *gladiators*; the one receives wounds, but yet maintains his ground, the other tells the people, when he is in blood, that *it is but a scratch*, and will not suffer anybody to part them. An *injury* cannot be received, but it must be *done*; but it may be *done* and yet not *received*; as a man may be in the water, and not swim, but if he swims, it is presumed that he is in the water. Or if a blow or a shot be levelled at us, it may so happen that a man may miss his aim, or some accident interpose that may divert the mischief. That which is hurt is passive, and inferior to that which hurts it. But you will say, that Socrates was condemned and put to death, and so received an injury; but I answer, that the tyrants *did* him an injury, and yet he *received* none. He that steals anything from me and hides it in my own house, though I have not lost it, yet he has stolen it. He that lies with his own wife, and takes her for another woman, though the woman be honest, the man is an adulterer. Suppose a man gives me a draught of poison and it proves not strong enough to kill me, his guilt is nevertheless for the disappointment. He that makes a pass at me is as much a murderer, though I put it by, as if he had struck me to the heart. It is the intention, not the effect, that makes the wickedness. He is a thief that has the will of killing and slaying, before his hand is dipt in blood; as it is sacrilege, the very intention of laying violent hands upon holy things. If a philosopher be exposed to torments, the ax over his head, his body wounded, his guts in his hands, I will allow him to groan; for virtue itself cannot divest him of the nature of a man; but if his mind stand firm, he has discharged his part. A great mind enables a man to maintain his station with honor; so that he only makes use of what he meets in his way, as a pilgrim that would fain be at his journey's end.

It is the excellency of a great mind to *ask* nothing, and to *want* nothing; and to say, "I will have nothing to do with fortune, that repulses Cato, and prefers Vatinius." He that quits his hold, and accounts anything good that is not honest, runs gaping after casualties, spends his days in anxiety and vain expectation, that man is miserable. And yet it is hard, you will say, to be banished or cast into prison: nay, what if it were to be burnt, or any other way destroyed? We have examples in all ages and cases, of great men that have triumphed over all misfortunes. Metellus suffered exile resolutely, Rutilius cheerfully; Socrates disputed in the dungeon; and though he might have made his escape, refused it; to show the world how easy a thing it was to subdue the two great terrors of mankind, *death* and a *jail*. Or what shall we say of Mucius Scevola, a man only of a military courage, and without the help either of philosophy or letters? who, when he found that he had killed the Secretary instead of Porsenna, (the prince,) burnt his right hand to ashes for the mistake; and held his arm in the flame until it was taken away by his very enemies. Porsenna did more easily pardon Mucius for his intent to kill him than Mucius forgave *himself* for missing of his aim. He might have a luckier thing, but never a braver.

Did not Cato, in the last night of his life, take Plato to bed with him, with his sword at his bed's head; the one that he might have death at his will, the other, that he might have it in his power; being resolved that no man should be able to say, either that he killed or that he saved Cato? So soon as he had composed his thoughts, he took his sword; "Fortune," says he, "I have hitherto fought for my country's liberty, and for my own, and only that I might live free among freemen; but the cause is now lost, and Cato safe." With that word he cast himself upon his sword; and after the physicians that pressed in upon him had bound up his wound, he tore it up again, and expired with the same greatness of soul that he lived. But these are the examples, you will say, of men famous in their generations.

Let us but consult history, and we shall find, even in the most effeminate of nations, and the most dissolute of times, men of all degrees, ages, and fortunes, nay, even women themselves, that have overcome the fear of death: which, in truth, is so little to be feared, that duly considered, it is one of the greatest benefits of nature. It was as great an honor for Cato, when his party was broken, that he himself stood his ground, as it would have been if he had carried the day, and settled an universal peace: for, it is an equal prudence, to make the best of a bad game, and to manage a good one. The day that he was *repulsed*, he *played*, and the night that he *killed* himself, he *read*, as valuing the loss of his life, and the missing of an office at the same rate. People, I know, are apt to pronounce upon other men's infirmities by the measure of their own, and to think it impossible that a man should be content to be burnt, wounded, killed, or shackled, though in some cases he may. It is only for a great mind to judge of great things; for otherwise, that which is our infirmity will seem to be another body's, as a straight stick in the water appears to be crooked: he that yields, draws upon his own head his own ruin; for we are sure to get the better of Fortune, if we do but struggle with her. Fencers and wrestlers, we see what blows and bruises they endure, not only for honor, but for exercise. If we turn our backs once, we are routed and pursued; that man only is happy that draws good out of evil, that stands fast in his judgment, and unmoved by any external violence; or however, so little moved, that the keenest arrow in the quiver of Fortune is but as the prick of a needle to him rather than a wound; and all her other weapons fall upon him only as hail upon the roof of a house, that crackles and skips off again, without any damage to the inhabitant.

A generous and clear-sighted young man will take it for a happiness to encounter ill fortune. It is nothing for a man to hold up his head in a calm; but to maintain his post when all others have quitted their ground, and there to stand upright where other men are beaten down, this is divine and praiseworthy. What ill is there in torments, or in those things which we commonly account grievous crosses? The great evil is the want of courage, the bowing and submitting to them, which can never happen to a wise man; for he stands upright under any weight; nothing that is to be borne displeases him; he knows his strength, and whatsoever may be any man's lot, he never complains of, if it be his own. Nature, he says, deceives nobody; she does not tell us whether our children shall be fair or foul, wise or foolish, good subjects or traitors, nor whether our fortune shall be good or bad. We must not judge of a man by his ornaments, but strip him of all the advantages and the impostures of Fortune, nay, of his very body too, and look into his mind. If he can see a naked sword at his eyes without so much as winking; if he make it a thing indifferent to him whether his life go out at his throat or at his mouth; if he can hear himself sentenced to torments or exiles, and under the very hand of the executioner, says thus to himself, "All this I am provided for, and it is no more than a man that is to suffer the fate of humanity." This is the temper of mind that speaks a man happy; and without this, all the confluences of external comforts signify no more than the personating of a king upon the stage; when the curtain is drawn, we are players again.

Not that I pretend to exempt a wise man out of a number of men, as if he had no sense of pain; but I reckon him as compounded of body and soul; the body is irrational, and may be galled, burnt, tortured; but the rational part is fearless, invincible, and not to be shaken. This it is that I reckon upon as the supreme good of man; which until it be perfected, is but an unsteady agitation of thought, and in the perfection an immovable stability. It is not in our contentions with Fortune as in those of the theatre, where we may throw down our arms, and pray for quarter; but here we must die firm and resolute. There needs no encouragement to those things which we are inclined to by a natural instinct, as the preservation of ourselves with ease and pleasure; but if it comes to the trial of our faith by torments, or of our courage by wounds, these are difficulties that we must be armed against by philosophy and precept; and yet all this is no more than what we were born to, and no matter of wonder at all; so that a wise man prepares himself for it, as expecting whatsoever *may be, will be*. My body is frail, and liable not only to the impressions of violence, but to afflictions also, that naturally succeed our pleasures. Full meals bring crudities; whoring and drinking make the hands to shake and the knees to tremble. It is only the surprise and newness of the thing which makes that misfortune terrible, which, by premeditation, might be made easy to us: for that which some people make light by sufferance, others do by foresight. Whatsoever is necessary, we must bear patiently. It is no new thing to die, no new thing to mourn, and no new thing to be merry again. Must I be *poor*? I shall have company: in *banishment*? I will think myself born there. If I *die*, I shall be no more sick; and it is a thing I cannot do but once.

Let us never wonder at anything we are born to; for no man has reason to complain, where we are all in the same condition. He that escapes might have suffered; and it is but equal to submit to the law of mortality. We must undergo the colds of winter, the heats of summer; the distempers of the air, and the diseases of the body. A wild beast meets us in one place, and a man that is more brutal in another; we are here assaulted by fire, there by water. Demetrius was reserved by Providence for the age he lived in, to show, that neither the times could corrupt him, nor he reform the people. He was a man of an exact judgment, steady to his purpose, and of a strong eloquence; not finical in his words, but his sense was masculine and vehement. He was so qualified in his life and discourse, that he served both for an example and a reproach. If fortune should have offered that man the government and possession of the whole world, upon condition not to lay it down again, I dare say he would have refused it: and thus have expostulated the matter with you: "Why should you tempt a freeman to put his shoulder under a burden; or an honest man to pollute himself with the dregs of mankind? Why do you offer me the spoils of princes, and of nations, and the price not only of your blood, but of your souls?"

It is the part of a great mind to be temperate in prosperity, resolute in adversity; to despise what the vulgar admire, and to prefer a mediocrity to an excess. Was not Socrates oppressed with poverty, labor, nay, the worst of wars in his own family, a fierce and turbulent woman for his wife? were not his children indocile, and like their mother? After seven-and-twenty years spent in arms, he fell under a slavery to the *thirty tyrants*, and most of them his bitter enemies: he came at last to be sentenced as "a violater of religion, a corrupter of youth, and a common enemy to God and man." After this he was imprisoned, and put to death by poison, which was all so far from working upon his mind, that it never so much as altered his countenance. We are to bear ill accidents as unkind seasons, distempers, or diseases; and why may we not reckon the actions of wicked men even among those accidents; their deliberations are not counsels but frauds, snares, and inordinate motions of the mind; and they are never without a thousand pretences and occasions of doing a man mischief. They have their informers, their knights of the post; they can make an interest with powerful men, and one may be robbed as well upon the bench as upon the highway. They lie in wait for advantages, and live in perpetual agitation betwixt hope and fear; whereas he that is truly composed will stand all shocks, either of violences, flatteries, or menaces, without perturbation. It is an inward fear that makes us curious after what we hear abroad.

It is an error to attribute either *good* or *ill* to *Fortune*; but the *matter* of it we may; and we ourselves are the occasion of it, being in effect the artificers of our own happiness or misery: for the mind is above fortune; if that be evil, it makes everything else so too; but if it be right and sincere, it corrects what is wrong, and mollifies what is hard, with modesty and courage. There is a great difference among those that the world calls wise men. Some take up private resolutions of opposing Fortune, but they cannot go through with them; for they are either dazzled with splendor on the one hand, or affrighted with terrors on the other; but there are others that will close and grapple with Fortune, and still come off victorious.

Mucius overcame the fire; Regulus, the gibbet; Socrates, poison; Rutilius, banishment; Cato, death; Fabricius, riches; Tubero, poverty; and Sextius, honors. But there are some again so delicate, that they cannot so much as bear a scandalous report; which is the same thing as if a man should quarrel for being jostled in a crowd, or dashed as he walks in the streets. He that has a great way to go must expect a slip, to stumble, and to be tired. To the luxurious man frugality is a punishment; labor and industry to the sluggard; nay, study itself is a torment to him; not that these things are hard to us by nature, but we ourselves are vain and irresolute; nay, we wonder many of us, how any man can live without wine, or endure to rise so early in a morning.

A brave man must expect to be tossed; for he is to steer his course in the teeth of Fortune, and to work against wind and weather. In the suffering of torments, though there appears but one virtue, a man exercises many. That which is most eminent is patience, (which is but a branch of fortitude.) But there is prudence also in the choice of the action, and in the bearing what we cannot avoid; and there is constancy in bearing it resolutely: and there is the same concurrence also of several virtues in other generous undertakings.

When Leonidas was to carry his 300 men into the Straits of Thermopylæ, to put a stop to Xerxes's huge army: "Come, fellow-soldiers," says he, "eat your dinners here as if you were to sup in another world." And they answered his resolution. How plain and imperious was that short speech of Cæditius to his men upon a desperate action! and how glorious a mixture was there in it both of bravery and prudence! "Soldiers," says he, "it is necessary for us to go, but it is not necessary for us to return." This brief and pertinent harangue was worth ten thousand of the frivolous cavils and distinctions of the schools, which rather break the mind than fortify it; and when it is once perplexed and pricked with difficulties and scruples, there they leave it. Our passions are numerous and strong, and not to be mastered with quirks and tricks, as if a man should undertake to defend the cause of God and man with a bulrush. It was a remarkable piece of honor and policy together, that action of Cæsar's upon the taking of Pompey's cabinet at the battle of Pharsalia: it is probable that the letters in it might have discovered who were his friends, and who his enemies; and yet he burnt it without so much as opening it; esteeming it the noblest way of pardoning, to keep himself ignorant both of the offender and of the offense. It was a brave presence of mind also in Alexander, who, upon advice that his physician Philip intended to poison him, took the letter of advice in one hand and the cup in the other; delivering Philip the letter to read while he himself drank the potion.

Some are of opinion that death gives a man courage to support pain, and that pain fortifies a man against death: but I say rather, that a wise man depends upon himself against both, and that he does not either suffer with patience, in hopes of death, or die willingly, because he is weary of life; but he bears the one, and waits for the other, and carries a divine mind through all the accidents of human life. He looks upon faith and honesty as the most sacred good of mankind, and neither to be forced by necessity nor corrupted by reward; kill, burn, tear him in pieces, he will be true to his trust; and the more any man labors to make him discover a secret, the deeper will he hide it. Resolution is the inexpugnable defence of human weakness, and it is a wonderful Providence that attends it.

Horatius Cocles opposed his single body to the whole army until the bridge was cut down behind him and then leaped into the river with his sword in his hand and came off safe to his party. There was a fellow questioned about a plot upon the life of a tyrant, and put to the torture to declare his confederates: he named, by one and one, all the tyrant's friends that were about him: and still as they were named, they were put to death: the tyrant asked him at last if there were any more. "Yes," says he, "yourself were in the plot; and now you have never another friend left in the world:" whereupon the tyrant cut the throats of his own guards. "He is the happy man that is the master of himself, and triumphs over the fear of death, which has overcome the conquerors of the world."

CHAPTER XVII.
OUR HAPPINESS DEPENDS IN A GREAT MEASURE UPON THE CHOICE OF OUR COMPANY.

The comfort of life depends upon conversation. Good offices, and concord, and human society, is like the working of an arch of stone; all would fall to the ground if one piece did not support another. Above all things let us have a tenderness for blood; and it is yet too little not to hurt, unless we profit one another. We are to relieve the distressed; to put the wanderer into his way; and to divide our bread with the hungry: which is but the doing of good to ourselves; for we are only several members of one great body. Nay, we are all of a consanguinity; formed of the same materials, and designed to the same end; this obliges us to a mutual tenderness and converse; and the other, to live with a regard to equity and justice. The love of society is natural; but the choice of our company is matter of virtue and prudence. Noble examples stir us up to noble actions; and the very history of large and public souls, inspires a man with generous thoughts. It makes a man long to be in action, and doing something that the world may be the better for; as protecting the weak, delivering the oppressed, punishing the insolent. It is a great blessing the very conscience of giving a good example; beside, that it is the greatest obligation any man can lay upon the age he lives in.

He that converses with the proud shall be puffed up; a lustful acquaintance makes a man lascivious; and the way to secure a man from wickedness is to withdraw from the examples of it. It is too much to have them *near* us, but more to have them *within* us – ill examples, pleasure and ease, are, no doubt of it, great corrupters of manners.

A rocky ground hardens the horse's hoof; the mountaineer makes the best soldier; the miner makes the best pioneer, and severity of discipline fortifies the mind. In all excesses and extremities of good and of ill fortune, let us have recourse to great examples that have contemned both. "These are the best instructors that teach in their lives, and prove their words by their actions."

As an ill air may endanger a good constitution, so may a place of ill example endanger a good man, nay, there are some places that have a kind of privilege to be licentious, and where luxury and dissolution of manners seem to be lawful; for great examples give both authority and excuse to wickedness. Those places are to be avoided as dangerous to our manners. Hannibal himself was unmanned by the looseness of Campania, and though a conqueror by his arms, he was overcome by his pleasures. I would as soon live among butchers as among cooks – not but a man may be temperate in any place – but to see drunken men staggering up and down everywhere, and only the spectacle of lust, luxury and excess before our eyes, it is not safe to expose ourselves to the temptation. If the victorious Hannibal himself could not resist it, what shall become of us then that are subdued, and give ground to our lusts already? He that has to do with an enemy in his breast, has a harder task upon him than he that is to encounter one in the field; his hazard is greater if he loses ground, and his duty is perpetual, for he has no place or time for rest. If I give way to pleasure, I must also yield to grief, to poverty, to labor, ambition, anger, until I am torn to pieces by my misfortunes and lusts. But against all this philosophy propounds a liberty, that is to say, a liberty from the service of accidents and fortune. There is not anything that does more mischief to mankind than mercenary masters and philosophy, that do not live as they teach – they give a scandal to virtue. How can any man expect that a ship should steer a fortunate course, when the pilot lies wallowing in his own vomit? It is a usual thing first to learn to do ill ourselves, and then to instruct others to do so: but that man must needs be very wicked that has gathered into himself the wickedness of other people.

The best conversation is with the philosophers – that is to say, with such of them as teach us matter, not words – that preach to us things necessary and keep us to the practice of them. There can be no peace in human life without the contempt of all events. There is nothing that either puts better thoughts into a man, or sooner sets him right that is out of the way, than a good companion, for the example has the force of a precept, and touches the heart with an affection to goodness; and not only the frequent hearing and seeing of a wise man delights us, but the very encounter of him suggests profitable contemplation such as a man finds himself moved with when he goes into a holy place. I will take more care with *whom* I eat and drink than *what*, for without a friend the table is a manger.

Writing does well, but personal discourse and conversation does better; for men give great credit to their ears, and take stronger impressions from example than precept. Cleanthes had never hit Zeno so to the life if he had not been in with him at all his privacies, if he had not watched and observed him whether or not he practised as he taught. Plato got more from Socrates' *manners* than from his *words*, and it was not the *school*, but the *company* and *familiarity* of Epicurus that made Metrodorus, Hermachus and Polyænus so famous.

Now, though it be by instinct that we covet society, and avoid solitude, we should yet take this along with us, that the more acquaintance the more danger: nay, there is not one man of a hundred that is to be trusted with himself. If company cannot alter us, it may interrupt us, and he that so much as stops upon the way loses a great deal of a short life, which we yet make shorter by our inconstancy. If an enemy were at our heels, what haste should we make! – but death is so, and yet we never mind it. There is no venturing of tender and easy natures among the people, for it is odds that they will go over to the major party. It would, perhaps, shake the constancy of Socrates, Cato, Lælius, or any of us all, even when our resolutions are at the height, to stand the shock of vice that presses upon us with a kind of public authority.

It is a world of mischief that may be done by one single example of avarice or luxury. One voluptuous palate makes a great many. A wealthy neighbor stirs up envy, and a fleering[4] companion moves ill-nature wherever he comes. What will become of those people then that expose themselves to a popular violence? which is ill both ways; either if they comply with the wicked, because they are many, or quarrel with the multitude because they are not principled alike. The best way is to retire, and associate only with those that may be the better for us, and we for them. These respects are mutual; for while we teach, we learn. To deal freely, I dare not trust myself in the hands of much company: I never go abroad that I come home again the same man I went out. Something or other that I had put in order is discomposed; some passion that I had subdued gets head again; and it is just with our minds as it is after a long indisposition with our bodies; we are grown so tender, that the least breath of air exposes us to a relapse. And it is no wonder if a numerous conversation be dangerous, where there is scarce any single man but by his discourse, example, or behavior, does either recommend to us, or imprint in us, or, by a kind of contagion, insensibly infect us with one vice or other; and the more people the greater is the peril. Especially let us have a care of public spectacles where wickedness insinuates itself with pleasure; and, above all others, let us avoid spectacles of cruelty and blood; and have nothing to do with those that are perpetually whining and complaining; there may be faith and kindness there, but no peace. People that are either sad or fearful, we do commonly, for their own sakes, set a guard upon them, for fear they should make an ill use of being alone; especially the imprudent, who are still contriving of mischief, either for others or for themselves, in cherishing their lusts, or forming their designs. So much for the choice of a *companion*; we shall now proceed to that of a *friend*.

---

4. *scoffing, taunting*

CHAPTER XVIII.
THE BLESSINGS OF FRIENDSHIP.

Of all felicities, the most charming is that of a *firm* and *gentle friendship*. It sweetens all our cares, dispels our sorrows, and counsels us in all extremities. Nay, if there were no other comfort in it than the bare exercise of so generous a virtue, even for that single reason, a man would not be without it. Beside, that it is a sovereign antidote against all calamities, even against the fear of death itself.

But we are not to number our friends by the *visits* that are made us; and to confound the decencies of *ceremony* and *commerce* with the offices of *united affections*. Caius Gracchus, and after him Livius Drusus, were the men that introduced among the Romans the fashion of separating their visitants; some were taken into their *closet*, others were only admitted into the *antechamber*: and some, again, were fain to wait in the *hall* perhaps, or in the *court*. So that they had their *first*, their *second*, and their *third rate* friends; but none of them true: only they are called so in course, as we salute strangers with some title or other of respect at a venture. There is no depending upon those men that only take their compliment in their turn, and rather slip through the door than enter at it. He will find himself in a great mistake, that either seeks for a friend in a palace, or tries him at a feast.

The great difficulty rests in the choice of him; that is to say, in the first place, let him be virtuous, for vice is contagious, and there is no trusting the sound and the sick together; and he ought to be a wise man too, if a body knew where to find him; but in this case, he that is least ill is best, and the highest degree of human prudence is only the most venial folly. That friendship where men's affections are cemented by an equal and by a common love of goodness, it is not either hope or fear, or any private interest, that can ever dissolve it: but we carry it with us to our graves, and lay down our lives for it with satisfaction. Paulina's good and mine (says our author) were so wrapped up together, that in consulting her comfort I provided for my own; and when I could not prevail upon her to take less care for me, she prevailed upon me to take more care for myself.

Some people make it a question, whether is the greatest delight, the enjoying of an old friendship, or the acquiring of a new one? but it is in the preparing of a friendship, and in the possession of it, as it is with the husbandman in sowing and reaping; his delight is the hope of his labor in the one case, and the fruit of it in the other. My conversation lies among my books, but yet in the letters of a friend, methinks I have his company; and when I answer them, I do not only write, but speak: and, in effect, a friend is an eye, a heart, a tongue, a hand, at all distances. When friends see one another personally, they do not see one another as they do when they are divided, where the meditation dignifies the prospect; but they are effectually in a great measure absent even when they are present. Consider their nights apart, their private studies, their separate employments, and necessary visits; and they are almost as much together divided as present. True friends are the whole world to one another; and he that is a friend to himself is also a friend to mankind. Even in my very studies, the greatest delight I take in what I learn is the teaching of it to others; for there is no relish, methinks, in the possession of anything without a partner; nay, if wisdom itself were offered me upon condition only of keeping it to myself, I should undoubtedly refuse it.

Lucilius tells me, that he was written to by a friend, but cautions me withal not to say anything to him of the affair in question; for he himself stands upon the same guard. What is this but to affirm and to deny the same thing in the same breath, in calling a man a friend, whom we dare not trust as our own soul? For there must be no reserves in friendship: as much deliberation as you please before the league is struck, but no doubtings or jealousies after. It is a preposterous weakness to love a man before we know him, and not to care for him after. It requires time to consider of a friendship, but the resolution once taken, entitles him to my very heart. I look upon my thoughts to be as safe in his breast as in my own: I shall, without any scruple, make him the confidant of my most secret cares and counsels.

It goes a great way toward the making of a man faithful, to let him understand that you think him so: and he that does but so much as suspect that I will deceive him gives me a kind of right to cozen him. When I am with my friend, methinks I am alone, and as much at liberty to speak anything as to think it, and as our hearts are one, so must be our interest and convenience; for friendship lays all things in common, and nothing can be good to the one that is ill to the other. I do not speak of such a community as to destroy one another's propriety; but as the father and the mother have two children, not one apiece, but each of them two.

But let us have a care, above all things, that our kindness be rightfully founded; for where there is any other invitation to friendship than the friendship itself, that friendship will be bought and sold. He derogates upon the majesty of it that makes it only dependent upon good fortune. It is a narrow consideration for a man to please himself in the thought of a friend, "because," says he, "I shall have one to help me when I am sick, in prison, or in want." A brave man should rather take delight in the contemplation of doing the same offices for another. He that loves a man for his own sake is in an error. A friendship of interest cannot last any longer than the interest itself, and this is the reason that men in prosperity are so much followed, and when a man goes down the wind, nobody comes near him.

Temporary friends will never stand the test. One man is forsaken for fear of profit, another is betrayed. It is a negotiation, not a friendship, that has an eye to advantages; only, through the corruption of times, that which was formerly a friendship is now become a design upon a booty: alter your testament, and you lose your friend. But my end of friendship is to have one dearer to me than myself, and for the saving of whose life I would cheerfully lay down my own; taking this along with me, that only wise men can be friends, others are but companions; and that there is a great difference also betwixt love and friendship; the one may sometimes do us hurt, the other always does us good, for the one friend is hopeful to another in all cases, as well in prosperity as in affliction. We receive comfort, even at a distance, from those we love, but then it is light and faint; whereas, presence and conversation touch us to the quick, especially if we find the man we love to be such a person as we wish.

It is usual with princes to reproach the living by commending the dead, and to praise those people for speaking truth from whom there is no longer any danger of hearing it. This is Augustus's case: he was forced to banish his daughter Julia for her common and prostituted impudence; and still upon fresh informations, he was often heard to say, "If Agrippa or Mecenas had been now alive, this would never have been." But yet where the fault lay may be a question; for perchance it was his own, that had rather complain for the want of them than seek for others as good. The Roman losses by war and by fire, Augustus could quickly supply and repair; but for the loss of two friends he lamented his whole life after.

Xerxes, (a vain and a foolish prince) when he made war upon Greece, one told him, "It would never come to a battle"; another, "That he would find only empty cities and countries, for they would not so much as stand the very fame of his coming;" others soothed him in the opinion of his *prodigious numbers*; and they all concurred to puff him up to his destruction; only Damaratus advised him not to depend too much upon his numbers, for he would rather find them a burden to him than an advantage: and that three hundred men in the straits of the mountains would be sufficient to give a check to his whole army; and that such an accident would undoubtedly turn his vast numbers to his confusion. It fell out afterward as he foretold, and he had thanks for his fidelity. A miserable prince, that among so many thousand subjects had but one servant to tell him the truth!

CHAPTER XIX.
HE THAT WOULD BE HAPPY MUST TAKE AN ACCOUNT OF HIS TIME.

In the distribution of human life, we find that a great part of it passes away in *evil doing*; a greater yet in doing just *nothing at all*: and effectually the whole in doing things *beside our business*. Some hours we bestow upon ceremony and servile attendances; some upon our pleasures, and the remainder runs at waste. What a deal of time is it that we spend in hopes and fears, love and revenge, in balls, treats, making of interests, suing for offices, soliciting of causes, and slavish flatteries! The shortness of life, I know, is the common complaint both of fools and philosophers; as if the time we have were not sufficient for our duties. But it is with our lives as with our estates, a good husband makes a little go a great way; whereas, let the revenue of a prince fall into the hands of a prodigal, it is gone in a moment. So that the time allotted us, if it were well employed, were abundantly enough to answer all the ends and purposes of mankind. But we squander it away in avarice, drink, sleep, luxury, ambition, fawning addresses, envy, rambling, voyages, impertinent studies, change of counsels, and the like; and when our portion is spent, we find the want of it, though we gave no heed to it in the passage: insomuch, that we have rather *made* our life short than *found* it so.

You shall have some people perpetually playing with their fingers, whistling, humming, and talking to themselves; and others consume their days in the composing, hearing, or reciting of songs and lampoons. How many precious morning hours do we spend in consultation with barbers, tailors, and tire-women, patching and painting betwixt the comb and the glass! A council must be called upon every hair we cut; and one curl amiss is as much as a body's life is worth. The truth is, we are more solicitous about our dress than our manners, and about the order of our periwigs than that of the government. At this rate, let us but discount, out of a life of a hundred years, that time which has been spent upon popular negotiations, frivolous amours, domestic brawls, sauntering up and down to no purpose, diseases that we have brought upon ourselves, and this large extent of life will not amount perhaps to the minority of another man. It is a long *being*, but perchance a *short* life. And what is the reason of all this? We live as we should never die, and without any thought of human frailty, when yet the very moment we bestow upon this man or thing, may, peradventure, be our last. But the greatest loss of time is delay and expectation, which depend upon the future. We let go the present, which we have in our own power; we look forward to that which depends upon Fortune; and so quit a certainty for an uncertainty. We should do by time as we do by a torrent, make use of it while we have it, for it will not last always.

The calamities of human nature may be divided into the *fear of death* and the *miseries and errors of life*. And it is the great work of mankind to master the one, and to rectify the other; and so live as neither to make life irksome to us, nor death terrible. It should be our care, before we are old, to live well, and when we are so, to die well; that we may expect our end without sadness: for it is the duty of life to prepare ourselves for death; and there is not an hour we live that does not mind us of our mortality.

Time runs on, and all things have their fate, though it lies in the dark. The period is certain to nature, but what am I the better for it if it be not so to me? We propound travels, arms, adventures, without ever considering that death lies in the way. Our term is set, and none of us know how near it is; but we are all of us agreed that the decree is unchangeable. Why should we wonder to have that befall us to-day which might have happened to us any minute since we were born? Let us therefore live as if every moment were to be our last, and set our accounts right every day that passes over our heads. We are not ready for death, and therefore we fear it, because we do not know what will become of us when we are gone, and that consideration strikes us with an inexplicable terror. The way to avoid this distraction is to contract our business and our thoughts – when the mind is once settled, a day or an age is all one to us; and the series of time, which is now our trouble will be then our delight; for he that is steadily resolved against all uncertainties, shall never be disturbed with the variety of them. Let us make haste, therefore, to live, since every day to a wise man is a new life – for he has done his business the day before, and so prepared himself for the next, that if it be not his last, he knows yet that it might have been so. No man enjoys the true taste of life but he that is willing and ready to quit it.

The wit of man is not able to express the blindness of human folly in taking so much more care of our fortunes, our houses, and our money, than we do of our lives – everybody breaks in upon the one *gratis*, but we betake ourselves to fire and sword if any man invades the other. There is no dividing in the case of patrimony, but people share our time with us at pleasure, so profuse are we of that only thing whereof we may be honestly covetous. It is a common practice to ask an hour or two of a friend for such or such a business, and it is as easily granted, both parties only considering the occasion, and not the thing itself. They never put time to account, which is the most valuable of all precious things; but because they do not see it they reckon upon it as nothing: and yet these easy men when they come to die would give the whole world for those hours again which they so inconsiderately cast away before; but there is no recovering of them. If they could number their days that are yet to come as they can those that are already past, how would those very people tremble at the apprehension of death, though a hundred years hence, that never so much as think of it at present, though they know not but it may take them away the next immediate minute!

It is an usual saying "I would give my life for such or such a friend," when, at the same time, we do give it without so much as thinking of it; nay, when that friend is never the better for it, and we ourselves the worse. Our time is set, and day and night we travel on. There is no baiting by the way, and it is not in the power of either prince or people to prolong it. Such is the love of life, that even those decrepit dotards that have lost the use of it will yet beg the continuance of it, and make themselves younger than they are, as if they could cozen even Fate itself! When they fall sick, what promises of amendment if they escape that bout! What exclamations against the folly of their misspent time – and yet if they recover, they relapse. No man takes care to live well, but long; when yet it is in everybody's power to do the former, and in no man's to do the latter. We consume our lives in providing the very instruments of life, and govern ourselves still with a regard to the future, so that we do not properly live, but we are about to live. How great a shame is it to be laying new foundations of life at our last gasp, and for an old man (that can only prove his age by his beard,) with one foot in the grave, to go to school again! While we are young we may learn; our minds are tractable and our bodies fit for labor and study; but when age comes on, we are seized with languor and sloth, afflicted with diseases, and at last we leave the world as ignorant as we came into it – only we *die* worse than we were *born*, which is none of Nature's fault, but ours; for our fears, suspicions, perfidy, etc., are from ourselves.

I wish with all my soul that I had thought of my end sooner, but I must make the more haste now and spur on like those that set out late upon a journey – it will be better to learn late than not at all – though it be but only to instruct me how I may leave the stage with honor.

In the division of life, there is time *present, past*, and *to come*. What we *do* is *short*, what we *shall do* is *doubtful*, but what we *have done* is *certain*, and out of the power of fortune. The passage of time is wonderfully quick, and a man must look backward to see it; and, in that retrospect, he has all past ages at a view; but the present gives us the slip unperceived. It is but a moment that we live, and yet we are dividing it into *childhood, youth, man's estate*, and *old age*, all which degrees we bring into that narrow compass. If we do not watch, we lose our opportunities; if we do not make haste, we are left behind; our best hours escape us, the worst are to come. The purest part of our life runs first, and leaves only the dregs at the bottom; and "that time which is good for nothing else, we dedicate to virtue;" and only propound to begin to live at an age that very few people arrive at. What greater folly can there be in the world than this loss of time, the future being so uncertain, and the damages so irreparable? If death be necessary, why should any man fear it? and if the time of it be uncertain, why should not we always expect it? We should therefore first prepare ourselves by a virtuous life against the dread of an inevitable death; and it is not for us to put off being good until such or such a business is over, for one business draws on another, and we do as good as sow it, one grain produces more. It is not enough to philosophize when we have nothing else to do, but we must attend wisdom even to the neglect of all things else; for we are so far from having time to spare, that the age of the world would be yet too narrow for our business; nor is it sufficient not to omit it, but we must not so much as intermit it.

There is nothing that we can properly call our own but our time, and yet every body fools us out of it that has a mind to it. If a man borrows a paltry sum of money, there must be bonds and securities, and every common civility is charged upon account; but he that has my time, thinks he owes me nothing for it, though it be a debt that gratitude itself can never repay. I cannot call any man poor that has enough still left, be it never so little: it is good advice yet to those that have the world before them, to play the good husbands betimes, for it is too late to spare at the bottom, when all is drawn out to the lees.

He that takes away a day from me, takes away what he can never restore me. But our time is either *forced away* from us, or *stolen* from us, or *lost*; of which the last is the foulest miscarriage. It is in life as in a journey; a book or a companion brings us to our lodging before we thought we were half-way. Upon the whole matter we consume ourselves one upon another, without any regard at all to our own particular. I do not speak of such as live in notorious scandal, but even those men themselves, whom the world pronounces happy, are smothered in their felicities, servants to their professions and clients, and drowned in their lusts. We are apt to complain of the haughtiness of *great men*, when yet there is hardly any of them all so proud but that, at some time or other, a man may yet have access to him, and perhaps a good word or look into the bargain. Why do we not rather complain of *ourselves*, for being of all others, even to ourselves, the most deaf and inaccessible.

Company and business are great devourers of time, and our vices destroy our lives as well as our fortunes. The present is but a moment, and perpetually in flux; the time past, we call to mind when we please, and it will abide the examination and inspection. But the busy man has not leisure to look back, or if he has, it is an unpleasant thing to reflect upon a life to be repented of, whereas the conscience of a good life puts a man into a secure and perpetual possession of a felicity never to be disturbed or taken away: but he that has led a wicked life is afraid of his own memory; and, in the review of himself, he finds only appetite, avarice, or ambition, instead of virtue. But still, he that is not at leisure many times to live, must, when his fate comes, whether he will or not, be at leisure to die. Alas! what is time to eternity? the age of a man to the age of the world? And how much of this little do we spend in fears, anxieties, tears, childhood! nay, we sleep away the one half. How great a part of it runs away in luxury and excess: the ranging of our guests, our servants, and our dishes! As if we were to eat and drink not for satiety, but ambition. The nights may well seem short that are so dear bought, and bestowed upon wine and women; the day is lost in expectation of the night, and the night in the apprehension of the morning. There is a terror in our very pleasures; and this vexatious thought in the very height of them, that *they will not last always*: which is a canker in the delights, even of the greatest and the most fortunate of men.

CHAPTER XX.
HAPPY IS THE MAN THAT MAY CHOOSE HIS OWN BUSINESS.

Oh the blessings of privacy and leisure! The wish of the powerful and eminent, but the privilege only of inferiors; who are the only people that live to themselves: nay, the very thought and hope of it is a consolation, even in the middle of all the tumults and hazards that attend greatness. It was Augustus' prayer, that he might live to retire and deliver himself from public business: his discourses were still pointing that way, and the highest felicity which this mighty prince had in prospect, was the divesting himself of that illustrious state, which, how glorious soever in show, had at the bottom of it only anxiety and care. But it is one thing to retire for pleasure, and another thing for virtue, which must be active even in that retreat, and give proof of what it has learned: for a good and a wise man does in privacy consult the well-being of posterity. Zeno and Chrysippus did greater things in their studies than if they had led armies, borne offices, or given laws; which in truth they did, not to one city alone, but to all mankind: their *quiet* contributed more to the common benefit than the *sweat* and *labor* of other people. That retreat is not worth the while which does not afford a man greater and nobler work than business. There is no slavish attendance upon great officers, no canvassing for places, no making of parties, no disappointments in my pretension to this charge, to that regiment, or to such or such a title, no envy of any man's favor or fortune; but a calm enjoyment of the general bounties of Providence in company with a good conscience. A wise man is never so busy as in the solitary contemplation of God and the works of Nature. He withdraws himself to attend the service of future ages: and those counsels which he finds salutary to himself, he commits to writing for the good of after-times, as we do the receipts of sovereign antidotes or balsams. He that is well employed in his study, though he may seem to do nothing at all, does the greatest things yet of all others, in affairs both human and divine. To supply a friend with a sum of money, or give my voice for an office, these are only private and particular obligations: but he that lays down precepts for the governing of our lives and the moderating of our passions, obliges human nature not only in the present, but in all succeeding generations.

He that would be at quiet, let him repair to his philosophy, a study that has credit with all sorts of men. The eloquence of the bar, or whatsoever else addresses to the people, is never without enemies; but philosophy minds its own business, and even the worst have an esteem for it. There can never be such a conspiracy against virtue, the world can never be so wicked, but the very name of a *philosopher* shall still continue venerable and sacred. And yet philosophy itself must be handled modestly and with caution. But what shall we say of Cato then, for his meddling in the broil of a civil war, and interposing himself in the quarrel betwixt two enraged princes? He that, when Rome was split into *two factions* betwixt Pompey and Cæsar, declared himself against *both*. I speak this of Cato's last part; for in his former time the commonwealth was made unfit for a wise man's administration. All he could do then was but bawling and beating of the air: one while he was lugged and tumbled by the rabble, spit upon and dragged out of the *forum*, and then again hurried out of the senate-house to prison. There are some things which we propound originally, and others which fall in as accessory to another proposition. If a wise man retire, it is no matter whether he does it because the commonwealth was wanting to him, or because he was wanting to it. But to what republic shall a man betake himself? Not to Athens, where Socrates was condemned, and whence Aristotle fled, for fear he should have been condemned too, and where virtue was oppressed by envy: not to Carthage, where there was nothing but tyranny, injustice, cruelty, and ingratitude. There is scarce any government to be found that will either endure a wise man, or which a wise man will endure; so that privacy is made necessary, because the only thing which is better is nowhere to be had. A man may commend navigation, and yet caution us against those seas that are troublesome and dangerous: so that he does as good as command me not to weigh anchor that commends sailing only upon these terms. He that is a slave to business is the most wretched of slaves.

"But how shall I get myself at liberty? We can run any hazards for money: take any pains for honor; and why do we not venture also something for leisure and freedom? without which we must expect to live and die in a tumult: for so long as we live in public, business breaks in upon us, as one billow drives on another; and there is no avoiding it with either modesty or quiet." It is a kind of whirlpool, that sucks a man in, and he can never disengage himself. A man of business cannot in truth be said to live, and not one of a thousand understands how to do it: for how to live, and how to die, is the lesson of every moment of our lives: all other arts have their masters.

As a busy life is always a miserable life, so it is the greatest of all miseries to be perpetually employed upon *other people's business*; for to sleep, to eat, to drink, at their hour; to walk their pace, and to love and hate as they do, is the vilest of servitudes. Now, though business must be quitted, let it not be done unseasonably; the longer we defer it, the more we endanger our liberty; and yet we must no more fly before the time than linger when the time comes: or, however, we must not love business for business' sake, nor indeed do we, but for the profit that goes along with it: for we love the reward of misery, though we hate the misery itself. Many people, I know, seek business without choosing it, and they are even weary of their lives without it for want of entertainment in their own thoughts; the hours are long and hateful to them when they are alone, and they seem as short on the other side in their debauches. When they are no longer *candidates*, they are s*uffragants*; when they give over other people's business, they do their own; and pretend business, but they make it, and value themselves upon being thought men of employment.

Liberty is the thing which they are perpetually a-wishing, and never come to obtain: a thing never to be bought nor sold, but a man must ask it of himself, and give it to himself. He that has given proof of his virtue in public, should do well to make a trial of it in private also. It is not that solitude, or a country life, teaches innocence or frugality; but vice falls of itself, without witnesses and spectators, for the thing it designs is to be taken notice of. Did ever any man put on rich clothes not to be seen? or spread the pomp of his luxury where nobody was to take notice of it? If it were not for admirers and spectators there would be no temptations to excess: the very keeping of us from exposing them cures us of desiring them, for vanity and intemperance are fed with ostentation.

He that has lived at sea in a storm, let him retire and die in the haven; but let his retreat be without ostentation, and wherein he may enjoy himself with a good conscience, without the want, the fear, the hatred, or the desire, of anything, not out of malevolent detestation of mankind, but for satisfaction and repose. He that shuns both business and men, either out of envy, or any other discontent, his retreat is but to the life of a mole: nor does he live to himself, as a wise man does, but to his bed, his belly, and his lusts. Many people seem to retire out of a weariness of public affairs, and the trouble of disappointments; and yet ambition finds them out even in that recess into which fear and weariness had cast them; and so does luxury, pride, and most of the distempers of a public life.

There are many that lie close, not that they may live securely, but that they may transgress more privately: it is their conscience, not their states, that makes them keep a porter; for they live at such a rate, that to be seen before they be aware is to be detected. Crates saw a young man walking by himself; "Have a care," says he "of lewd company." Some men are busy in idleness, and make peace more laborious and troublesome than war; nay, and more wicked too, when they bestow it upon such lusts, and other vices, which even the license of a military life would not endure. We cannot call these people men of leisure that are wholly taken up with their pleasures.

A troublesome life is much to be preferred before a slothful one; and it is a strange thing, methinks, that any man should fear death that has buried himself alive; as privacy without letters is but the burying of a man quick.

There are some that make a boast of their retreat, which is but a kind of lazy ambition; they retire to make people talk of them, whereas I would rather withdraw to speak to myself. And what shall that be, but that which we are apt to speak of one another? I will speak ill of myself: I will examine, accuse, and punish my infirmities. I have no design to be cried up for a great man, that has renounced the world in a contempt of the vanity and madness of human life; I blame nobody but myself, and I address only to myself. He that comes to me for help is mistaken, for I am not a physician, but a patient: and I shall be well enough content to have it said, when any man leaves me, "I took him for a happy and a learned man, and truly I find no such matter." I had rather have my retreat pardoned than envied.

There are some creatures that confound their footing about their dens, that they may not be found out, and so should a wise man in the case of his retirement. When the door is open, the thief passes it by as not worth his while; but when it is bolted and sealed, it is a temptation for people to be prying. To have it said "that such a one is never out of his study, and sees nobody," etc.; this furnishes matter for discourse. He that makes his retirement too strict and severe, does as good as call company to take notice of it.

Every man knows his own constitution; one eases his stomach by vomit – another supports it with good nourishment; he that has the gout forbears wine and bathing, and every man applies to the part that is most infirm. He that shows a gouty foot, a lame hand, or contracted nerves, shall be permitted to lie still and attend his cure; and why not so in the vices of his mind! We must discharge all impediments and make way for philosophy, as a study inconsistent with common business. To all other things we must deny ourselves openly and frankly, when we are sick we refuse visits, keep ourselves close, and lay aside all public cares, and shall we not do as much when we philosophize? Business is the drudgery of the world, and only fit for slaves, but contemplation is the work of wise men. Not but that solitude and company may be allowed to take their turns: the one creates in us the love of mankind, the other that of ourselves; solitude relieves us when we are sick of company, and conversation when we are weary of being alone; so that the one cures the other. "There is no man," in fine, "so miserable as he that is at a loss how to spend his time." He is restless in his thoughts, unsteady in his counsels, dissatisfied with the present, solicitous for the future; whereas he that prudently computes his hours and his business, does not only fortify himself against the common accidents of life, but improves the most rigorous dispensations of Providence to his comfort, and stands firm under all the trials of human weakness.

CHAPTER XXI.
THE CONTEMPT OF DEATH MAKES ALL THE MISERIES OF LIFE EASY TO US.

It is a hard task to master the natural desire of life by a philosophical contempt of death, and to convince the world that there is no hurt in it, and crush an opinion that was brought up with us from our cradles. What help? what encouragement? what shall we say to human frailty, to carry it fearless through the fury of flames, and upon the points of swords? What rhetoric shall we use to bear down the universal consent of people to so dangerous an error? The captious and superfine subtleties of the schools will never do the work: these speak many things sharp, but utterly unnecessary, and void of effect. The truth of it is, there is but one chain that holds all the world in bondage, and that is the love of life. It is not that I propound the making of death so indifferent to us, as it is, whether a man's hairs be even or odd; for what with self-love, and an implanted desire in every being of preserving itself, and a long acquaintance betwixt the soul and body, friends may be loth to part, and death may carry an appearance of evil, though in truth it is itself no evil at all. Beside, that we are to go to a strange place in the dark, and under great uncertainties of our future state; so that people die in terror, because they do not know whither they are to go, and they are apt to fancy the worst of what they do not understand: these thoughts are indeed sufficient to startle a man of great resolution without a wonderful support from above. And, moreover, our natural scruples and infirmities are assisted by the wits and fancies of all ages, in their infamous and horrid description of another world: nay, taking it for granted that there will be no reward and punishment, they are yet more afraid of an annihilation than of hell itself.

But what is it we fear? "Oh! it is a terrible thing to die." Well; and is it not better once to suffer it, than always to fear it? The earth itself suffers both *with* me, and *before* me. How many islands are swallowed up in the sea! how many towns do we sail over! nay, how many nations are wholly lost, either by inundations or earthquakes! and shall I be afraid of my little body? why should I, that am sure to die, and that all other things are mortal, be fearful of coming to my last gasp myself? It is the fear of death that makes us base, and troubles and destroys the life we would preserve; that aggravates all circumstances, and makes them formidable. We depend but upon a flying moment. Die we must; but when? what is that to us? It is the law of Nature, the tribute of mortals, and the remedy of all evils. It is only the disguise that affrights us; as children that are terrified with a vizor. Take away the instruments of death, the fire, the ax, the guards, the executioners, the whips, and the racks; take away the pomp, I say, and the circumstances that accompany it, and death is no more than what my slave yesterday contemned; the pain is nothing to a fit of the stone; if it be tolerable, it is not great; and if intolerable, it cannot last long. There is nothing that Nature has made necessary which is more easy than death: we are longer a-coming into the world than going out of it; and there is not any minute of our lives wherein we may not reasonably expect it. Nay, it is but a moment's work, the parting of the soul and body. What a shame is it then to stand in fear of anything so long that is over so soon!

Nor is it any great matter to overcome this fear; for we have examples as well of the *meanest* of men as of the greatest that have done it. There was a fellow to be exposed upon the theatre, who in disdain thrust a stick down his own throat, and choked himself; and another on the same occasion, pretended to nod upon the chariot, as if he were asleep, cast his head betwixt the spokes of the wheel, and kept his seat until his neck was broken. Caligula, upon a dispute with Canius Julius; "Do not flatter yourself," says he, "for I have given orders to put you to death." "I thank your most gracious Majesty for it," says Canius, giving to understand, perhaps, that under his government death was a mercy: for he knew that Caligula seldom failed of being as good as his word in that case. He was at play when the officer carried him away to his execution, and beckoning to the centurion, "Pray," says he, "will you bear me witness, when I am dead and gone, that I had the better of the game?" He was a man exceedingly beloved and lamented, and, for a farewell, after he had preached moderation to his friends; "You," says he, "are here disputing about the immortality of the soul, and I am now going to learn the truth of it. If I discover any thing upon that point, you shall hear of it." Nay, the most timorous of creatures, when they see there is no escaping, they oppose themselves to all dangers; the despair gives them courage, and the necessity overcomes the fear. Socrates was thirty days in prison after his sentence, and had time enough to have starved himself, and so to have prevented the poison: but he gave the world the blessing of his life as long as he could, and took that fatal draught in the meditation and contempt of death.

Marcellinus, in a deliberation upon death, called several of his friends about him: one was fearful, and advised what he himself would have done in the case; another gave the counsel which he thought Marcellinus would like best; but a friend of his that was a Stoic, and a stout man, reasoned the matter to him after this manner; Marcellinus do not trouble yourself, as if it were such a mighty business that you have now in hand; it is nothing to *live*; all your servants do it, nay, your very beasts too; but to die honestly and resolutely, that is a great point. Consider with yourself there is nothing pleasant in life but what you have tasted already, and that which is to come is but the same over again; and how many men are there in the world that rather choose to die than to suffer the nauseous tediousness of the repetition? Upon which discourse he fasted himself to death. It was the custom of Pacuvius to solemnize, in a kind of pageantry, every day his own funeral. When he had swilled and gormandized to a luxurious and beastly excess, he was carried away from supper to bed with this song and acclamation, "He has lived, he has lived." That which he did in lewdness, will become us to do in sobriety and prudence. If it shall please God to add another day to our lives, let us thankfully receive it; but, however, it is our happiest and securest course so to compose ourselves to-night, that we may have no anxious dependence on to-morrow. "He that can say, I have lived this day, makes the next clear again."

Death is the worst that either the severity of laws or the cruelty of tyrants can impose upon us; and it is the utmost extent of the dominion of Fortune. He that is fortified against that, must, consequently, be superior to all other difficulties that are put in the way to it. Nay, and on some occasions, it requires more courage to live than to die. He that is not prepared for death shall be perpetually troubled, as well with vain apprehensions, as with real dangers. It is not death itself that is dreadful, but the fear of it that goes before it. When the mind is under a consternation, there is no state of life that can please us; for we do not so endeavor to avoid mischiefs as to run away from them, and the greatest slaughter is upon a flying enemy. Had not a man better breathe out his last once for all, than lie agonizing in pains, consuming by inches, losing of his blood by drops? and yet how many are there that are ready to betray their country, and their friends, and to prostitute their very wives and daughters, to preserve a miserable carcass! Madmen and children have no apprehension of death; and it were a shame that our reason should not do as much toward our security as their folly. But the great matter is to die considerately and cheerfully upon the foundation of virtue; for life in itself is irksome, and only eating and drinking in a circle.

How many are there that, betwixt the apprehensions of death and the miseries of life, are at their wits' end what to do with themselves? Wherefore let us fortify ourselves against those calamities from which the prince is no more exempt than the beggar. Pompey the Great had his head taken off by a boy and a eunuch, (young Ptolemy and Photinus.) Caligula commanded the tribune Dæcimus to kill Lepidus; and another tribune (Chæreus) did as much for Caligula. Never was a man so great but he was as liable to suffer mischief as he was able to do it. Has not a thief, or an enemy, your throat at his mercy? nay, and the meanest of servants has the power of life and death over his master; for whosoever contemns his own life may be master of another body's. You will find in story, that the displeasure of servants has been as fatal as that of tyrants: and what matters it the power of him we fear, when the thing we fear is in every body's power? Suppose I fall into the hands of an enemy, and the conqueror condemns me to be led in triumph;

it is but carrying me thither whither I should have gone without him, that is to say, toward death, whither I have been marching ever since I was born. It is the fear of our last hour that disquiets all the rest. By the justice of all constitutions, mankind is condemned to a capital punishment; now, how despicable would that man appear, who, being sentenced to death in common with the whole world, should only petition that he might be the last man brought to the block?

Some men are particularly afraid of thunder, and yet extremely careless of other and of greater dangers: as if that were all they have to fear. Will not a sword, a stone, a fever, do the work as well? Suppose the bolt should hit us, it were yet braver to die with a stroke than with the bare apprehension of it: beside the vanity of imagining that heaven and earth should be put into such a disorder only for the death of one man. A good and a brave man is not moved with lightning, tempest, or earthquakes; but perhaps he would voluntarily plunge himself into that gulf, where otherwise he should only fall. The cutting of a corn, or the swallowing of a fly, is enough to dispatch a man; and it is no matter how great that is that brings me to my death, so long as death itself is but little. Life is a small matter; but it is a matter of importance to contemn it. Nature, that begat us, expels us, and a better and a safer place is provided for us. And what is death but a ceasing to be what we were before? We are kindled and put out: to cease to be, and not to begin to be, is the same thing. We die daily, and while we are growing, our life decreases; every moment that passes takes away part of it; all that is past is lost; nay, we divide with death the very instant that we live. As the last sand in the glass does not measure the hour, but finishes it; so the last moment that we live does not make up death, but concludes. There are some that pray more earnestly for death than we do for life; but it is better to receive it cheerfully when it comes than to hasten it before the time.

"But what is it that we would live any longer for?" Not for our pleasures; for those we have tasted over and over, even to satiety: so that there is no point of luxury that is new to us. "But a man would be loth to leave his country and his friends behind him;" that is to say, he would have them go first; for that is the least part of his care. "Well; but I would fain live to do more good, and discharge myself in the offices of life;" as if to die were not the duty of every man that lives. We are loth to leave our possessions; and no man swims well with his luggage. We are all of us equally fearful of death, and ignorant of life; but what can be more shameful than to be solicitous upon the brink of security? If death be at any time to be feared, it is always to be feared; but the way never to fear it, is to be often thinking of it. To what end is it to put off for a little while that which we cannot avoid? He that dies does but follow him that is dead. "Why are we then so long afraid of that which is so little awhile of doing?" How miserable are those people that spend their lives in the dismal apprehensions of death!

for they are beset on all hands, and every minute in dread of a surprise. We must therefore look about us, as if we were in an enemy's country; and consider our last hour, not as a punishment, but as the law of Nature: the fear of it is a continual palpitation of the heart, and he that overcomes that terror shall never be troubled with any other.

Life is a navigation; we are perpetually wallowing and dashing one against another; sometimes we suffer shipwreck, but we are always in danger and in expectation of it. And what is it when it comes, but either the end of a journey, or a passage? It is as great a folly to fear *death* as to fear *old age*; nay, as to fear life itself; for he that would not die ought not to live, since death is the condition of life. Beside that it is a madness to fear a thing that is certain; for where there is no doubt, there is no place for fear.

We are still chiding of Fate, and even those that exact the most rigorous justice betwixt man and man are yet themselves unjust to Providence. "Why was such a one taken away in the prime of his years?" As if it were the number of years that makes death easy to us, and not the temper of the mind. He that would live a little longer to-day, would be as loth to die a hundred years hence. But which is more reasonable for us to obey Nature, or for Nature to obey us? Go we must at last, and no matter how soon. It is the work of Fate to make us live long, but it is the business of virtue to make a short life sufficient. Life is to be measured by action, not by time; a man may die old at thirty, and young at fourscore: nay, the one lives after death, and the other perished before he died. I look upon age among the effects of chance. How long I shall live is in the power of others, but it is in my own how well. The largest space of time is to live till a man is wise. He that dies of old age does no more than go to bed when he is weary. Death is the test of life, and it is that only which discovers what we are, and distinguishes betwixt ostentation and virtue. A man may dispute, cite great authorities, talk learnedly, huff it out, and yet be rotten at heart. But let us soberly attend our business: and since it is uncertain *when*, or *where*, we shall die, let us look for death in all places, and at all times: we can never study that point too much, which we can never come to experiment whether we know it or not. It is a blessed thing to dispatch the business of life before we die, and then to expect death in the possession of a happy life. He is the great man who is willing to die when his life is pleasant to him. An honest life is not a greater good than an honest death. How many brave young men, by an instinct of Nature, are carried on to great actions, and even to the contempt of all hazards!

It is childish to go out of the world groaning and wailing as we came into it. Our bodies must be thrown away, as the secundine[5] that wraps up the infant, the other being only the covering of the soul; we shall then discover the secrets of

---

5. *the afterbirth*

Nature; the darkness shall be discussed, and our souls irradiated with light and glory: a glory without a shadow; a glory that shall surround us, and from whence we shall look down and see day and night beneath us. If we cannot lift up our eyes toward the lamp of heaven without dazzling, what shall we do when we come to behold the divine light in its illustrious original? That death which we so much dread and decline, is not the determination, but the intermission of a life, which will return again. All those things, that are the very cause of life, are the way to death: we fear it as we do fame; but it is a great folly to fear words. Some people are so impatient of life, that they are still wishing for death; but he that wishes to die does not desire it: let us rather wait God's pleasure, and pray for health and life. If we have a mind to live, why do we wish to die? If we have a mind to die, we may do it without talking of it. Men are a great deal more resolute in the article of *death* itself than they are about the circumstances of it: for it gives a man courage to consider that his fate is inevitable: the slow approaches of death are the most troublesome to us; as we see many a gladiator, who upon his wounds, will direct his adversary's weapon to his very heart, though but timorous perhaps in the combat. There are some that have not the heart either to live or die; that is a sad case. But this we are sure of, "the fear of death is a continual slavery, as the contempt of it is certain liberty."

CHAPTER XXII.
CONSOLATIONS AGAINST DEATH, FROM THE PROVIDENCE AND THE NECESSITY OF IT.

This life is only a prelude to eternity, where we are to expect another original, and another state of things; we have no prospect of heaven here but at a distance; let us therefore expect our last and decretory hour with courage. The last (I say) to our bodies, but not to our minds: our luggage we leave behind us, and return as naked out of the world as we came into it. The day which we fear as our last is but the birth-day of our eternity; and it is the only way to it. So that what we fear as a rock, proves to be but a port, in many cases to be desired, never to be refused; and he that dies young has only made a quick voyage of it. Some are becalmed, others cut it away before wind; and we live just as we sail: first, we rub our childhood out of sight; our youth next; and then our middle age: after that follows old age, and brings us to the common end of mankind.

It is a great providence that we have more ways out of the world than we have into it. Our security stands upon a point, the very article of death. It draws a great many blessings into a very narrow compass: and although the fruit of it does not seem to extend to the defunct, yet the difficulty of it is more than balanced by the contemplation of the future. Nay, suppose that all the business of this world should be forgotten, or my memory, traduced, what is all this to me? "I have done my duty." Undoubtedly that which puts an end to all other evils, cannot be a very great evil itself, and yet it is no easy thing for flesh and blood to despise life. What if death comes? If it does not stay with us why should we fear it? One hangs himself for a mistress; another leaps the garret-window to avoid a choleric master; a third runs away and stabs himself, rather than he will be brought back again. We see the force even of our infirmities, and shall we not then do greater things for the love of virtue? To suffer death is but the law of nature; and it is a great comfort that it can be done but once; in the very convulsions of it we have this consolation, that our pain is near an end, and that it frees us from all the miseries of life.

What it is we know not, and it were rash to condemn what we do not understand; but this we presume, either that we shall pass out of this into a better life, where we shall live with tranquillity and splendor, in diviner mansions, or else return to our first principles, free from the sense of any inconvenience. There is nothing immortal, nor many things lasting; by but divers ways everything comes to an end. What an arrogance is it then, when the world itself stands condemned to a dissolution, that man alone should expect to live forever! It is unjust not to allow unto the giver the power of disposing of his own bounty, and a folly only to value the present. Death is as much a debt as money, and life is but a journey towards it: some dispatch it sooner, others later, but we must all have the same period. The thunderbolt is undoubtedly just that draws even from those that are struck with it a veneration.

A great soul takes no delight in staying with the body: it considers whence it came, and knows whither it is to go. The day will come that shall separate this mixture of soul and body, of divine and human; my body I will leave where I found it, my soul I will restore to heaven, which would have been there already, but for the clog that keeps it down: and beside, how many men have been the worse for longer living, that might have died with reputation if they had been sooner taken away! How many disappointments of hopeful youths, that have proved dissolute men! Over and above the ruins, shipwrecks, torments, prisons, that attend long life; a blessing so deceitful, that if a child were in condition to judge of it, and at liberty to refuse it, he would not take it.

What Providence has made necessary, human prudence should comply with cheerfully: as there is a necessity of death, so that necessity is equal and invincible. No man has cause of complaint for that which every man must suffer as well as himself. When we *should* die, *we will* not, and when we *would not* we *must*: but our fate is fixed, and unavoidable is the decree. Why do we then stand trembling when the time comes? Why do we not as well lament that we did not live a thousand years ago, as that we shall not be alive a thousand years hence? It is but traveling the great road, and to the place whither we must all go at last. It is but submitting to the law of Nature, and to that lot which the whole world has suffered that is gone before us; and so must they too that are to come after us. Nay, how many thousands, when our time comes, will expire in the same moment with us! He that will not follow shall be drawn by force: and is it not much better now to do that willingly which we shall otherwise be made to do in spite of our hearts?

The sons of mortal parents must expect a mortal posterity – death is the end of great and small. We are born helpless, and exposed to the injuries of all creatures and of all weathers. The very necessaries of life are deadly to us; we meet with our fate in our dishes, in our cups, and in the very air we breathe; nay, our very birth is inauspicious, for we come into the world weeping, and in the middle of our designs, while we are meditating great matters, and stretching of our thoughts to after ages, death cuts us off, and our longest date is only the revolution of a few years. One man dies at the table; another goes away in his sleep, a third in his mistress's arms, a fourth is stabbed, another is stung with an adder, or crushed with the fall of a house. We have several ways to our end, but the end itself, which is death, is still the same. Whether we die by a sword, by a halter, by a potion, or by a disease, it is all but *death*. A child dies in the swaddling-clouts, and an old man at a hundred – they are both mortal alike, though the one goes sooner than the other. All that lies betwixt the cradle and the grave is uncertain. If we compute the *troubles*, the life even of a child is long: if the *sweetness* of the *passage*, that of an old man is short; the whole is slippery and deceitful, and only death certain; and yet all people complain of that which never deceived any man. Senecio raised himself from a small beginning to a vast fortune, being very well skilled in the faculties both of getting and of keeping, and either of them was sufficient for the doing of his business. He was a man infinitely careful both of his patrimony and of his body. He gave me a morning's visit, (says our author,) and after that visit he went away and spent the rest of the day with a friend of his that was desperately sick. At night, he was merry at supper, and seized immediately after with a quinsy which dispatched him in a few hours. This man that had money at use in all places, and in the very course and height of his prosperity was thus cut off. How foolish a thing is it then for a man to flatter himself with long hopes, and to pretend to dispose of the future: nay, the very present slips through our fingers, and there is not that moment which we can call our own.

How vain a thing is it for us to enter upon projects, and to say to ourselves, "Well, I will go build, purchase, discharge such offices, settle my affairs, and then retire!" We are all of us born to the same casualties – all equally frail and uncertain of to-morrow. At the very altar where we pray for life, we learn to die, by seeing the sacrifices killed before us. But there is no need of a wound, or searching the heart for it, when the noose of a cord, or the smothering of a pillow will do the work. All things have their seasons – they begin, they increase, and they die. The heavens and the earth grow old, and are appointed their periods.

That which we call *death* is but a pause or suspension; and, in truth, a progress to life, only our thoughts look downward upon the body, and not forward upon things to come. All things under the sun are mortal – cities – empires – and the time will come when it shall be a question where they were, and, perchance, whether ever they had a being or not. Some will be destroyed by war, others by luxury, fire, inundations, earthquakes – why should it trouble me then to die, as a forerunner of an universal dissolution? A great mind submits itself to God, and suffers willingly what the law of the universe will otherwise bring to pass upon necessity.

That good old man Bassus, (though with one foot in the grave,) how cheerful a mind does he bear. He lives in the view of death, and contemplates his own end with less concern of thought or countenance, than he would do another man's. It is a hard lesson, and we are a long time a learning of it, to receive our death without trouble, especially in the case of Bassus: in other deaths there is a mixture of hope – a disease may be cured, a fire quenched, a falling house either propped or avoided, the sea may swallow a man and throw him up again, a pardon may interpose twixt the axe and the body – but in the case of old age there is no place for either hope or intercession.

Let us live in our bodies, therefore, as if we were only to lodge in them this night, and to leave them to-morrow. It is the frequent thought of death that must fortify us against the necessity of it. He that has armed himself against poverty, may, perhaps, come to live in plenty. A man may strengthen himself against pain and yet live in a state of health; against the loss of friends, and never lose any, but he that fortifies himself against the fear of death shall most certainly have occasion to employ that virtue. It is the care of a wise and a good man to look to his manners and actions; and rather how well he lives than how long, for to die sooner or later is not the business, but to die well or ill, for "death brings us to immortality."

CHAPTER XXIII.
AGAINST IMMODERATE SORROW FOR THE DEATH OF FRIENDS.

Next to the encounter of death in our own bodies, the most sensible calamity to an honest man is the death of a friend; and we are not in truth without some generous instances of those that have preferred a friend's life before their own; and yet this affliction, which by nature is so grievous to us, is by virtue and Providence made familiar and easy.

To lament the death of a friend is both natural and just; a sigh or a tear I would allow to his memory: but no profuse or obstinate sorrow. Clamorous and public lamentations are not so much the effects of grief as of vain-glory. He that is sadder in company than alone, shows rather the ambition of his sorrow than the piety of it. Nay, and in the violence of his passion there fall out twenty things that set him a-laughing. At the long-run, time cures all, but it were better done by moderation and wisdom. Some people do as good as set a watch upon themselves, as if they were afraid that their grief would make an escape. The ostentation of grief is many times more than the grief itself. When any body is within hearing, what groans and outcries! when they are alone and private, all is hush and quiet: so soon as any body comes in, they are at it again; and down they throw themselves upon the bed; fall to wringing of their hands, and wishing of themselves dead; which they might have executed by themselves; but their sorrow goes off with the company.

We forsake nature, and run over to the practices of the people, that never were the authors of anything that is good. If destiny were to be wrought upon by tears, I would allow you to spend your days and nights in sadness and mourning, tearing of your hair, and beating of your breast; but if Fate be inexorable, and death will keep what it has taken, grief is to no purpose. And yet I would not advise insensibility and hardness; it were inhumanity, and not virtue, not to be moved at the separation of familiar friends and relations: now, in such cases, we cannot command ourselves, we cannot forbear weeping, and we ought not to forbear: but let us not pass the bounds of affection, and run into imitation; within these limits it is some ease to the mind.

A wise man gives way to tears in some cases, and cannot avoid them in others. When one is struck with the surprise of ill-news, as the death of a friend, or the like; or upon the last embrace of an acquaintance under the hand of an executioner, he lies under a natural necessity of weeping and trembling. In another case, we may indulge our sorrow, as upon the memory of a dead friend's conversation or kindness, one may let fall tears of generosity and joy. We favor the one, and we are overcome by the other; and this is well: but we are not upon any terms to force them: they may flow of their own accord, without derogating from the dignity of a wise man; who at the same time both preserves his gravity, and obeys nature. Nay, there is a certain *decorum* even in weeping; for excess of sorrow is as foolish as profuse laughter. Why do we not as well cry, when our trees that we took pleasure in, shed their leaves, as at the loss of our satisfactions; when the next season repairs them, either with the same again, or others in their places.

We may *accuse* Fate, but we cannot *alter* it; for it is hard and inexorable, and not to be removed either with reproaches or tears. They may carry *us* to the *dead*, but never bring *them* back again to us. If reason does not put an end to our sorrows, fortune never will: one is pinched with poverty; another solicited with ambition, and fears the very wealth that he coveted. One is troubled for the loss of children; another for the want of them: so that we shall sooner want tears than matter for them; let us therefore spare that for which we have so much occasion. I do confess, that in the very parting of friends there is something of uneasiness and trouble; but it is rather voluntary than natural; and it is custom more than sense that affects us: we do rather impose a sorrow upon ourselves than submit to it; as people cry when they have company, and when nobody looks on, all is well again. To mourn without measure is folly, and not to mourn at all is insensibility. The best temper is betwixt piety and reason; to be sensible, but neither transported nor cast down. He that can put a stop to his tears and pleasures when he will is safe. It is an equal infelicity to be either too soft or too hard: we are overcome by the one, and put to struggle with the other. There is a certain intemperance in that sorrow that passes the rules of modesty; and yet great piety is, in many cases, a dispensation to good manners. The loss of a son or of a friend, cuts a man to the heart, and there is no opposing the first violence of his passion; but when a man comes once to deliver himself wholly up to lamentations, he is to understand, that though some tears deserve compassion, others are yet ridiculous. A grief that is fresh finds pity and comfort, but when it is inveterate it is laughed at, for it is either counterfeit or foolish. Beside that, to weep excessively for the dead is an affront to the living.

The most justifiable cause of mourning is to see good men come to ill ends, and virtue oppressed by the iniquity of Fortune. But in this case, too, they either suffer resolutely, and yield us delight in their courage and example, or meanly, and so give us the less trouble for the loss. He that dies cheerfully, dries up my tears; and he that dies whiningly, does not deserve them. I would bear the death of friends and children with the same constancy that I would expect my own, and no more lament the one than fear the other.

He that bethinks himself, how often friends have been parted, will find more time lost among the living, than upon the dead; and the most desperate mourners are they that cared least for their friends when they were living; for they think to redeem their credits, for want of kindness to the living, by extravagant ravings after the dead. Some (I know) will have grief to be only the perverse delight of a restless mind, and sorrows and pleasures to be near akin; and there are, I am confident, that find joy even in their tears. But which is more barbarous, to be insensible of grief for the death of a friend, or to fish for pleasure in grief, when a son perhaps is burning, or a friend expiring? To forget one's friend, to bury the memory with the body, to lament out of measure, is all inhuman. He that is gone either would not have his friend tormented, or does not know that he is so: if he does not feel it, it is superfluous; if he does, it is unacceptable to him. If reason cannot prevail, reputation may; for immoderate mourning lessens a man's character: it is a shameful thing for a wise man to make the *weariness* of grieving the *remedy* of it. In time, the most stubborn grief will leave us, if in prudence we do not leave that first.

But do I grieve for my friend's sake or for my own? Why should I afflict myself for the loss of him that is either happy or not at all in being? In the one case it is envy, and in the other it is madness. We are apt to say, "What would I give to see him again, and to enjoy his conversation! I was never sad in his company: my heart leaped whenever I met him; I want him wherever I go." All that is to be said is, "The greater the loss, the greater is the virtue to overcome it." If grieving will do no good, it is an idle thing to grieve; and if that which has befallen one man remains to all, it is as unjust to complain. The whole world is upon the march towards the same point; why do we not cry for ourselves that are to follow, as well as for him that has gone first? Why do we not as well lament beforehand for that which we know will be, and can not possibly but be? He is not *gone*, but *sent before*. As there are many things that he has lost, so there are many things that he does not fear; as anger, jealousy, envy, etc. Is he not more happy in desiring nothing than miserable in what he has lost? We do not mourn for the absent, why then for the dead, who are effectually no other? We have lost one blessing, but we have many left; and shall not all these satisfactions support us against one sorrow?

The comfort of having a friend may be taken away, but not that of having had one. As there is a sharpness in some fruits, and a bitterness in some wines that please us, so there is a mixture in the remembrance of friends, where the loss of their company is sweetened again by the contemplation of their virtues. In some respects, I have lost what I had, and in others, I retain still what I have lost. It is an ill construction of Providence to reflect only upon my friend's being taken away, without any regard to the benefit of his being once given me. Let us therefore make the best of our friends while we have them; for how long we shall keep them is uncertain. I have lost a hopeful son, but how many fathers have been deceived in their expectations! and how many noble families have been destroyed by luxury and riot! He that grieves for the loss of a son, what if he had lost a friend? and yet he that has lost a friend has more cause of joy that he once had him, than of grief that he is taken away. Shall a man bury his friendship with his friend? We are ungrateful for that which is past, in hope of what is to come; as if that which is to come would not quickly be past too. That which is past we are sure of. We may receive satisfaction, it is true, both from the future and what is already past; the one by expectation, and the other by memory; only the one may possibly not come to pass, and it is impossible to make the other not to have been.

But there is no applying of consolation to fresh and bleeding sorrow; the very discourse irritates the grief and inflames it. It is like an unseasonable medicine in a disease; when the first violence is over, it will be more tractable, and endure the handling. Those people whose minds are weakened by long felicity may be allowed to groan and complain, but it is otherwise with those that have led their days in misfortunes. A long course of adversity has this good in it, that though it vexes a body a great while, it comes to harden us at last; as a raw soldier shrinks at every wound, and dreads the surgeon more than an enemy; whereas a *veteran* sees his own body cut and lamed with as little concern as if it were another's. With the same resolution should we stand the shock and cure of all misfortunes; we are never the better for our experience, if we have not yet learned to be miserable. And there is no thought of curing us by the diversion of sports and entertainments; we are apt to fall into relapses; wherefore we had better overcome our sorrow than delude it.

CHAPTER XXIV.
CONSOLATION AGAINST BANISHMENT AND BODILY PAIN.

It is a masterpiece to draw good out of evil; and, by the help of virtue, to improve misfortunes into blessings. "It is a sad condition," you will say, "for a man to be barred the freedom of his own country." And is not this the case of thousands that we meet every day in the streets? Some for ambition; others, to negotiate, or for curiosity, delight, friendship, study, experience, luxury, vanity, discontent: some to exercise their virtues, others their vices; and not a few to prostitute either their bodies or their eloquence? To pass now from pleasant countries into the worst of islands; let them be never so barren or rocky, the people never so barbarous, or the clime never so intemperate, he that is banished thither shall find many strangers to live there for their pleasure. The mind of man is naturally curious and restless; which is no wonder, considering their divine original; for heavenly things are always in motion: witness the stars, and the orbs, which are perpetually moving, rolling, and changing of place and according to the law and appointment of Nature. But here are no woods, you will say, no rivers, no gold nor pearl, no commodity for traffic or commerce; nay, hardly provision enough to keep the inhabitants from starving. It is very right; here are no palaces, no artificial grottoes, or materials for luxury and excess; but we lie under the protection of Heaven; and a poor cottage for a retreat is more worth than the most magnificent temple, when that cottage is consecrated by an honest man under the guard of his virtue. Shall any man think banishment grievous, when he may take such company along with him!

Nor is there any banishment but yields enough for our necessities, and no kingdom is sufficient for superfluities. It is the mind that makes us rich in a desert; and if the body be but kept alive, the soul enjoys all spiritual felicities in abundance. What signifies the being banished from one spot of ground to another, to a man that has his thoughts above, and can look forward and backward, and wherever he pleases; and that, wherever he is, has the same matter to work upon? The body is but the prison or the clog of the mind, subjected to punishments, robberies, diseases; but the mind is sacred and spiritual, and liable to no violence. Is it that, a man shall want garments or covering in banishment? The body is as easily clothed as fed; and Nature has made nothing hard that is necessary. But if nothing will serve us but rich embroideries and scarlet, it is none of Fortune's fault that we are poor, but our own. Nay, suppose a man should have all restored him back again that he has lost, it will come to nothing, for he will want more after that to satisfy his desires than he did before to supply his necessities. Insatiable appetites are not so much a thirst as a disease.

To come lower now; where is the people or nation that have not changed their place of abode? Some by the fate of war; others have been cast by tempests, shipwrecks, or want of provisions, upon unknown coasts. Some have been forced abroad by pestilence, sedition, earthquakes, surcharge of people at home. Some travel to see the world, others for commerce; but, in fine, it is clear, that, upon some reason or other, the whole race of mankind have shifted their quarters; changed their very names as well as their habitations; insomuch that we have lost the very memorials of what they were. All these transportations of people, what are they but public banishments? The very *founder* of the *Roman empire* was an *exile*: briefly, the whole world has been transplanted, and one mutation treads upon the heel of another. That which one man desires, turns another man's stomach; and he that proscribes me to-day, shall himself be cast out to-morrow. We have, however, this comfort in our misfortune; we have the same nature, the same Providence, and we carry our virtues along with us. And this blessing we owe to that almighty Power, call it what you will; either a *God*, or an *Incorporeal Reason*, a *Divine Spirit*, or *Fate*, and the *unchangeable Course of causes* and *effects*: it is, however, so ordered, that nothing can be taken from us but what we can well spare: and that which is most magnificent and valuable continues with us. Wherever we go, we have the heavens over our heads, and no farther from us than they were before; and so long as we can entertain our eyes and thoughts with those glories, what matter is it what ground we tread upon?

In the case of pain or sickness, it is only the body that is affected; it may take off the speed of a footman, or bind the hands of a cobbler, but the mind is still at liberty to hear, learn, teach, advise, and to do other good offices. It is an example of public benefit, a man that is in pain and patient. Virtue may show itself as well in the bed as in the field; and he that cheerfully encounters the terrors of death and corporal anguish, is as great a man as he that most generously hazards himself in a battle. A disease, it is true, bars us of some pleasures, but procures us others. Drink is never so grateful to us as in a burning fever; nor meat, as when we have fasted ourselves sharp and hungry. The patient may be forbidden some sensual satisfaction, but no physician will forbid us the delight of the mind. Shall we call any sick man miserable, because he must give over his intemperance of wine and gluttony, and betake himself to a diet of more sobriety, and less expense; and abandon his luxury, which is the distemper of the mind as well as of the body? It is troublesome, I know, at first, to abstain from the pleasures we have been used to, and to endure hunger and thirst; but in a little time we lose the very appetite, and it is no trouble then to be without that which we do not desire. In diseases there are great pains; but if they be long they remit, and give us some intervals of ease; if short and violent, either they dispatch *us*, or consume *themselves*; so that either their respites make them tolerable, or the extremity makes them short. So merciful is Almighty God to us, that our torments cannot be very sharp and lasting. The acutest pains are those that affect the nerves, but there is this comfort in them too, that they will quickly make us stupid and insensible. In cases of extremity, let us call to mind the most eminent instances of patience and courage, and turn our thoughts from our afflictions to the contemplation of virtue. Suppose it be the stone, the gout, nay, the rack itself; how many have endured it without so much as a groan or word speaking; without so much as asking for relief, or giving an answer to a question! Nay, they have laughed at the tormentors upon the very torture, and provoked them to new experiments of their cruelty, which they have had still in derision. The *asthma* I look upon as of all diseases the most importunate; the physicians call it the *meditation of death*, as being rather an agony than a sickness; the fit holds one not above an hour, as nobody is long in expiring. Are there not three things grievous in sickness, the fear of death, bodily pain, and the intermission of our pleasures? the first is to be imputed to nature, not to the disease; for we do not die because we are sick, but because we live. Nay, sickness itself has preserved many a man from dying.

CHAPTER XXV.
POVERTY TO A WISE MAN IS RATHER A BLESSING THAN A MISFORTUNE.

No man shall ever be poor that goes to himself for what he wants; and that is the readiest way to riches. Nature, indeed, will have her due; but yet whatsoever is beyond necessity is precarious, and not necessary. It is not her business to gratify the palate, but to satisfy a craving stomach. Bread, when a man is hungry, does his work, let it be never so coarse; and water when he is dry; let his thirst be quenched, and Nature is satisfied, no matter whence it comes, or whether he drinks in gold, silver, or in the hollow of his hand. To promise a man riches, and to teach him poverty, is to deceive him: but shall I call him poor that wants nothing; though he maybe beholden for it to his patience, rather than to his fortune? Or shall any man deny him to be rich, whose riches can never be taken away? Whether is it better to have much or enough? He that has much desires more, and shows that he has not yet enough; but he that has enough is at rest. Shall a man be reputed the less rich for not having that for which he shall be banished; for which his very wife, or son, shall poison him: that which gives him security in war, and quiet in peace; which he possesses without danger, and disposes of without trouble? No man can be poor that has enough; nor rich, that covets more than he has. Alexander, after all his conquests, complained that he wanted more worlds; he desired something more, even when he had gotten all: and that which was sufficient for human nature was not enough for one man. Money never made any man rich; for the more he had, the more he still coveted. The richest man that ever lived is poor in my opinion, and in any man's may be so: but he that keeps himself to the stint of Nature, does neither feel poverty nor fear it; nay, even in poverty itself there are some things superfluous. Those which the world calls happy, their felicity is a false splendor, that dazzles the eyes of the vulgar; but our rich man is glorious and happy within. There is no ambition in hunger or thirst: let there be food, and no matter for the table, the dish, and the servants, nor with what meats nature is satisfied. Those are the torments of luxury, that rather stuff the stomach than fill it: it studies rather to cause an appetite than to allay it. It is not for us to say, "This is not handsome; that is common; the other offends my eye." Nature provides for health, not delicacy. When the trumpet sounds a charge, the poor man knows that he is not aimed at; when they cry out *fire*, his body is all he has to look after: if he be to take a journey, there is no blocking up of streets, and thronging of passages, for a parting compliment: a small matter fills his belly, and contents his mind: he lives from hand to mouth, without caring or fearing for to-morrow. The temperate rich man is but his counterfeit; his wit is quicker and his appetite calmer.

No man finds poverty a trouble to him, but he that thinks it so; and he that thinks it so, makes it so. Does not a rich man travel more at ease with less luggage, and fewer servants? Does he not eat many times as little and as coarse in the field as a poor man? Does he not for his own pleasure, sometimes, and for variety, feed upon the ground, and use only earthen vessels? Is not he a madman then, that always fears what he often desires, and dreads the thing that he takes delight to imitate: he that would know the worst of poverty, let him but compare the looks of the rich and of the poor, and he shall find the poor man to have a smoother brow, and to be more merry at heart; or if any trouble befalls him, it passes over like a cloud: whereas the other, either his good humor is counterfeit, or his melancholy deep and ulcerated, and the worse, because he dares not publicly own his misfortune; but he is forced to play the part of a happy man even with a cancer in his heart. His felicity is but personated; and if he were but stripped of his ornaments, he would be contemptible. In buying of a horse, we take off his clothes and his trappings, and examine his shape and body for fear of being cozened; and shall we put an estimate upon a man for being set off by his fortune and quality? Nay, if we see anything of ornament about him, we are to suspect him the more for some infirmity under it. He that is not content in poverty, would not be so neither in plenty; for the fault is not in the thing, but in the mind. If that be sickly, remove him from a kennel to a palace, he is at the same pass; for he carries his disease along with him.

What can be happier than the condition both of mind and of fortune from which we cannot fall – what can be a greater felicity than in a covetous, designing age, for a man to live safe among informers and thieves? It puts a poor man into the very condition of Providence, that gives all, without reserving anything to itself. How happy is he that owes nothing but to himself, and only that which he can easily refuse or easily pay! I do not reckon him poor that has but a little, but he is so that covets more – it is a fair degree of plenty to have what is necessary. Whether had a man better find satiety in want, or hunger in plenty? It is not the augmenting of our fortunes, but the abating of our appetites that makes us rich.

Why may not a man as well contemn riches in his own coffers as in another man's, and rather hear that they are his than feel them to be so, though it is a great matter not to be corrupted even by having them under the same roof. He is the greater man that is honestly poor in the middle of plenty – but he is the more secure that is free from the temptation of that plenty, and has the least matter for another to design upon. It is no great business for a poor man to preach the contempt of riches, or for a rich man to extol the benefits of poverty, because we do not know how either the one or the other would behave himself in the contrary condition. The best proof is the doing of it by choice and not by necessity; for the practice of poverty in jest is a preparation toward the bearing of it in earnest; but it is yet a generous disposition so to provide for the worst of fortunes as what may be easily borne – the premeditation makes them not only tolerable but delightful to us, for there is that in them without which nothing can be comfortable, that is to say, security. If there were nothing else in poverty but the certain knowledge of our friends, it were yet a most desirable blessing, when every man leaves us but those that love us. It is a shame to place the happiness of life in gold and silver, for which bread and water is sufficient; or, at the worst, hunger puts an end to hunger.

For the honor of *poverty*, it was both the *foundation* and the *cause of the Roman empire*; and no man was ever yet so poor but he had enough to carry him to his journey's end.

All I desire is that my property may not be a burden to myself, or make me so to others; and that is the best state of fortune that is neither directly necessitous, nor far from it. A mediocricity of fortune with a gentleness of mind, will preserve us from fear or envy, which is a desirable condition, for no man wants power to do mischief. We never consider the blessing of coveting nothing, and the glory of being full in ourselves, without depending upon Fortune. With parsimony a little is sufficient and without it nothing; whereas frugality makes a poor man rich. If we lose an estate, we had better never have had it – he that has least to lose has least to fear, and those are better satisfied whom Fortune never favored, than those whom she has forsaken.

The state is most commodious that lies betwixt poverty and plenty. Diogenes understood this very well when he put himself into an incapacity of losing any thing. That course of life is most commodious which is both safe and wholesome – the body is to be indulged no farther than for health, and rather mortified than not kept in subjection to the mind. It is necessary to provide against hunger, thirst, and cold; and somewhat for a covering to shelter us against other inconveniences; but not a pin matter whether it be of turf or of marble – a man may lie as warm and as dry under a thatched as under a gilded roof.

Let the mind be great and glorious, and all other things are despicable in comparison. "The future is uncertain, and I had rather beg of myself not to desire any thing, than of Fortune to bestow it."

finis

SENECA: HIS LIFE - AND DEATH.

It has been an ancient custom to record the actions and the writings of eminent men, with all their circumstances, and it is but a rite that we owe to the memory of our famous author.

Lucius Annæus Seneca was by birth a Spaniard of Cordova, (a Roman colony of great fame and antiquity.), being born there circa 4 B.C. He was of the family of Annæus, of the order of knights; and the father, also named Lucius Annæus Seneca, was distinguished from the son by the name of *The Orator*. His mother's name was Helvia, a woman of excellent qualities.

His father came to Rome in the time of Augustus, and his wife and children soon followed him, our Seneca yet being in his infancy. There were three brothers of them, and never a sister: Marcus Annæus Novatus, Lucius Annæus Seneca, and Lucius Annæus Mela; the first of these changed his name for Junius Gallio, who adopted him; to him it was that Seneca dedicated his treatise *On Anger*, whom he calls Novatus too. He also dedicated this present discourse, *On a Happy Life,* to his brother Gallio. The youngest brother (Annæus Mela) was the father of the poet Lucan. Seneca was about twenty years of age in the fifth year of Tiberius, when the Jews were expelled from Rome.

His father trained him up to *rhetoric*, but his genius led him rather to *philosophy*; and he applied his wit to *morality* and *virtue*. In his youth he studied in the school of the Sextii, which blended Stoicism with an ascetic Neo-Pythagoreanism. He was a great hearer of the celebrated men of those times; as Attalus, Sotion, Papirius, Fabianus, (of whom he often makes mention,) and he was much an admirer also of Demetrius the Cynic, whose conversation he had afterwards in the Court, and both at home also and abroad, for they often travelled together. His father was not at all pleased with his humor of *philosophy*, but forced him upon the *law*, and for a while he practiced *pleading*. After which he would needs put him upon public employment: and he came first to be *quæstor*, then *prætor*, and some will have it that he was chosen *consul*; but this is doubtful.

Seneca's life at Rome was full of danger. Around 31 A.D., having returned from Egypt (whence he had travelled to recuperate from ill health) Emperor Caligula sought his death, and was only dissuaded from ordering his execution after being told that Seneca was so enfeebled his life was sure to be of brief duration. Some ten years later he was accused of adultery with the niece of the latest Emperor, Claudius, and was banished to the island of Corsica for eight long years. It was here he wrote his three-part *Consolationes* (Consolations). Recalled to Rome in AD 49, his fortunes improved when he married the wealthy Pompeia Paulina, and was appointed tutor to the princeling Nero.

The assassination of Claudius and accession of his pupil as Emperor bought

Seneca great power and prestige. His estate was partly patrimonial, but the greatest part of it was the bounty of his prince. His gardens, villas, lands, possessions, and incredible sums of money, are agreed upon at all hands; which drew an envy upon him. Dio reports him to have had £250,000 sterling at interest in Britanny alone, which he called in all at a sum. However, he seems, for the most part, to have held to his stoic philosophy and to have been an influence of restraint on Nero's arbitrary and cruel rule. The Court itself could not bring him to flattery; and for his piety, submission, and virtue, the practice of his whole life witnesses for him.

"So soon," says he, "as the candle is taken away, my wife, that knows my custom, lies still, without a word speaking, and then do I recollect all that I have said or done that day, and take myself to shrift. And why should I conceal or reserve anything, or make any scruple of inquiring into my errors, when I can say to myself, Do so no more, and for this once I will forgive thee?" And again, what can be more pious and self-denying than this passage, in one of his epistles? "Believe me now, when I tell you the very bottom of my soul: in all the difficulties and crosses of my life, this is my consideration – since it is God's will, I do not only obey, but assent to it; nor do I comply out of necessity, but inclination."

Later in Nero's rule, finding that he had ill offices done him at court, and that the Empeor's favor began to cool, Seneca went directly and resolutely to Nero, with an offer to refund all that he had gotten, which Nero would not receive. However, from that time on the philosopher changed his course of life, received few visits, shunned company, went little abroad; still pretending to be kept at home, either by indisposition or by his study. Being Nero's tutor and governor, all things were well so long as Nero followed his counsel. His two chief favorites were Burrhus and Seneca, who were both of them excellent in their ways: Burrhus, in his care of *military* affairs, and severity of *discipline*; Seneca for his *precepts* and *good advice* in the matter of *eloquence*, and the *gentleness* of an *honest mind*; assisting one another, in that slippery age of the prince (says Tacitus) to invite him, by the allowance of lawful pleasures, to the love of virtue. Seneca had two wives; the name of the first is not mentioned; his second was Paulina, whom he often speaks of with great passion. By the former he had his son Marcus.

"Here follows now," says Tacitus, "the death of Seneca, to Nero's great satisfaction; not so much for any pregnant proof against him that he was of Piso's conspiracy; but Nero was resolved to do that by the sword which he could not effect by poison. For it is reported, that Nero had corrupted Cleonicus (a freeman of Seneca's) to give his master poison, which did not succeed. Whether that the servant had discovered it to his master, or that Seneca, by his own caution and jealousy, had avoided it; for he lived only upon a simple diet, as the fruits of the earth, and his drink was most commonly river water.

"Natalis, it seems, was sent upon a visit to him (being indisposed) with a complaint that he would not let Piso come at him; and advising him to the continuance of their friendship and acquaintance as formerly. To whom Seneca made answer, that frequent meetings and conferences betwixt them could do neither of them any good; but that he had a great interest in Piso's welfare. Hereupon Granius Silvanus (a captain of the guard) was sent to examine Seneca upon the discourse that passed betwixt him and Natalis, and to return his answer. Seneca, either by chance or upon purpose, came that day from Campania, to a villa of his own, within four miles of the city; and thither the officer went the next evening, and beset the place.

He found Seneca at supper with his wife Paulina, and two of his friends; and gave him immediately an account of his commission. Seneca told him, that it was true that Natalis had been with him in Piso's name, with a complaint *that Piso could not be admitted to see him*; and that he excused himself by reason of his want of health, and his desires to be quiet and private; and that he had no reason to prefer another man's welfare before his own. Cæsar himself, he said, knew very well that he was not a man of compliment, having received more proofs of his freedom than of his flattery. This answer of Seneca's was delivered to Cæsar in the presence of Poppæa, and Tigellinus, the intimate confidants of this barbarous prince: and Nero asked him whether he could gather anything from Seneca as if he intended to make himself away? The tribune's answer was, that he did not find him one jot moved with the message: but that he went on roundly with his tale, and never so much as changed countenance for the matter. Go back to him then, says Nero, and tell him, *that he is condemned to die*. Fabius Rusticus delivers it, that the tribune did not return the same way he came, but went aside to Fenius (a captain of that name) and told him Cæsar's orders, asking his advice whether he should obey them or not; who bade him by all means to do as he was ordered. Which want of resolution was fatal to them all; for Silvanus also, that was one of the conspirators, assisted now to serve and to increase those crimes, which he had before complotted to revenge. And yet he did not think fit to appear himself in the business, but sent a centurion to Seneca to tell him his doom.

"Seneca, without any surprise or disorder, calls for his will; which being refused him by the officer, he turned to his friends, and told them that since he was not permitted to requite them as they deserved, he was yet at liberty to bequeath them the thing of all others that he esteemed the most, that is, the image of his life; which should give them the reputation both of *constancy* and *friendship*, if they would but imitate it; exhorting them to a firmness of mind, sometimes by good counsel, otherwhile by reprehension, as the occasion required. Where, says he, is all your philosophy now? all your *premeditated resolutions* against the violences of Fortune? Is there any man so ignorant of Nero's cruelty, as to expect, after the murder of his mother and his brother, that he should ever spare the life of his governor and tutor?

After some general expressions to this purpose, he took his wife in his arms, and having somewhat fortified her against the present calamity, he besought and conjured her to moderate her sorrows, and betake herself to the contemplations and comforts of a virtuous life; which would be a fair and ample consolation to her for the loss of her husband. Paulina, on the other side, tells him her determination to bear him company, and wills the executioner to do his office. Well, says Seneca, if after the sweetness of life, as I have represented it to thee, thou hadst rather entertain an honorable death, I shall not envy thy example; consulting, at the same time, the fame of the person he loved, and his own tenderness, for fear of the injuries that might attend her when he was gone. Our resolution, says he, in this generous act, may be equal, but thine will be the greater reputation. After this the veins of both their arms were opened at the same time. Seneca did not bleed so freely, his spirits being wasted with age and a thin diet; so that he was forced to cut the veins of his thighs and elsewhere, to hasten his dispatch.

When he was far spent, and almost sinking under his torments, he desired his wife to remove into another chamber, lest the agonies of the one might work upon the courage of the other. His eloquence continued to the last, as appears by the excellent things he delivered at his death; which being taken in writing from his own mouth, and published in his own words, I shall not presume to deliver them in any other. Nero, in the meantime, who had no particular spite to Paulina, gave orders to prevent her death, for fear his cruelty should grow more and more insupportable and odious. Whereupon the soldiers gave all freedom and encouragement to her servants to bind up her wounds, and stop the blood, which they did accordingly; but whether she was sensible of it or not is a question. For among the common people, who are apt to judge the worst, there were some of opinion, that as long as she despaired of Nero's mercy, she seemed to court the glory of dying with her husband for company; but that upon the likelihood of better quarter she was prevailed upon to outlive him; and so for some years she did survive him, with all piety and respect to his memory; but so miserably pale and wan, that everybody might read the loss of her blood and spirits in her very countenance.

"Seneca finding his death slow and lingering, desires Statius Annæus (his old friend and physician) to give him a dose of poison, which he had provided beforehand, being the same preparation which was appointed for capital offenders in Athens. This was brought him, and he drank it up, but to little purpose; for his body was already chilled, and bound up against the force of it. He went at last into a hot bath, and sprinkling some of his servants that were next him, this, says he, is an oblation to Jupiter *the deliverer*. The fume of the bath soon dispatched him, and his body was burnt, without any funeral solemnity, as he had directed in his testament: though this will of his was made in the height of his prosperity and power. There was a rumor that Subrius Flavius, in a private consultation with the centurions, had taken up this following resolution, (and that Seneca himself was no stranger to it) that is to say, that after Nero should have been slain by the help of Piso, Piso himself should have been killed too; and the empire delivered up to Seneca, as one that well deserved it, for his integrity and virtue."

AZILOTH BOOKS

Aziloth Books publishes a wide range of titles ranging from hard-to-find esoteric books - *Parchment Books* - to classic works on fiction, politics and philosophy - *Cathedral Classics*. Our newest venture is *Aziloth Books Children's Classics*, with vibrant new covers and illustrations to complement some of the world's very best children's tales. All our imprints are offered to the reader at a competitive price and through as many mediums and outlets as possible.

We are committed to excellent book production and strive, whenever possible, to add value to our titles with original images, maps and author introductions. With the premium on space in most modern dwellings, we also endeavour - within the limits of good book design - to make our products as slender as possible, allowing more books to be fitted into a given bookshelf area.

We are a small, approachable company and would love to hear any of your comments and suggestions on our plans, products, or indeed on absolutely anything.

Aziloth Books, Rimey Law, Rookhope, Co. Durham, DL13 2BL, England.
t: 01388-517600 e: info@azilothbooks.com w: www.azilothbooks.com

PARCHMENT BOOKS enshrines the concept of the oneness of all true religious traditions - that "the light shines from many different lanterns". Our list below offers titles from both eastern and western spiritual traditions, including Christian, Judaic, Islamic, Daoist, Hindu and Buddhist mystical texts, as well as books on alchemy, hermeticism, paganism, etc..

By bringing together such spiritual texts, we hope to make esoteric and occult knowledge more readily available to those ready to receive it. We do not publish grimoires or titles pertaining to the left hand path. Titles include:

The Prophet	Khalil Gibran
The Madman: His Parables & Poems	Khalil Gibran
Abandonment to Divine Providence	Jean-Pierre de Caussade
Corpus Hermeticum	G. R. S. Mead (trans.)
The Holy Rule of St Benedict	St. Benedict of Nursia
The Confession of St Patrick	St. Patrick
The Outline of Sanity	G. K. Chesterton
An Outline of Occult Science	Rudolf Steiner
The Dialogue Of St Catherine Of Siena	St. Catherine of Siena
Esoteric Christianity; Thought-Forms*	Annie Besant
The Teachings of Zoroaster	Shapurji A. Kapadia
The Spiritual Exercises of St. Ignatius	St. Ignatius of Loyola
Daemonologie	King James of England
A Dweller on Two Planets	Phylos the Thibetan
Bushido*	Nitobe Inazo
The Interior Castle	St. Teresa of Avila
Songs of Innocence & Experience*	William Blake
The Secret of the Rosary	St. Louis Marie de Montfort
From Ritual to Romance	Jessie L. Weston
The God of the Witches	Margaret Murray
Kundalini – an occult experience	George S. Arundale
The Kingdom of God is Within You	Leo Tolstoy
The Trial and Death of Socrates	Plato
A Textbook of Theosophy	Charles W. Leadbetter
Chuang Tzu: Daoist Teachings	Chuang Tzu
Practical Mysticism	Evelyn Underhill
Tao Te Ching (Lao Tzu's 'Book of the Way')	Tzu, Lao
The Most Holy Trinosophia	Le Comte de St.-Germain
Tertium Organum	P. D. Ouspensky
Totem and Taboo	Sigmund Freud
The Kebra Negast	E. A. Wallis Budge
Esoteric Buddhism	Alfred Percy Sinnett
Demian: the story of a youth	Hermann Hesse
Religio Medici	Thomas Browne
The Jefferson Bible	Thomas Jefferson
The Dhammapada	W. Wagiswara & K. Saunders

* with colour illustrations
Obtainable at all good online and local bookstores.
View Aziloth Books' full list at: www.azilothbooks.com

CATHEDRAL CLASSICS hosts an array of classic literature, from erudite ancient tomes to avant-garde, twentieth-century masterpieces, all of which deserve a place in your home. All the world's great novelists are here, Jane Austen, Dickens, Conrad, Arthur Machen and Henry James, brushing shoulders with such disparate luminaries as Sun Tzu, Marcus Aurelius, Kipling, Friedrich Nietzsche, Machiavelli, and Omar Khayam. A small selection is detailed below:

Frankenstein	Mary Shelley
Herland; With Her in Ourland	Charlotte Perkins Gilman
The Time Machine; The Invisible Man	H. G. Wells
Three Men in a Boat	Jerome K Jerome
The Rubaiyat of Omar Khayyam	Omar Khayyam
A Study in Scarlet	Arthur Conan Doyle
The Sign of the Four	Arthur Conan Doyle
The Picture of Dorian Gray	Oscar Wilde
Flatland	Edwin A. Abbott
The Coming Race	Bulwer Lytton
The Adventures of Sherlock Holmes	Arthur Conan Doyle
The Great God Pan	Arthur Machen
Beyond Good and Evil	Friedrich Nietzsche
England, My England	D. H. Lawrence
The Castle of Otranto	Horace Walpole
Self-Reliance, & Other Essays (series1&2)	Ralph W. Emmerson
The Art of War	Sun Tzu
A Shepherd's Life	W. H. Hudson
The Double	Fyodor Dostoyevsky
To the Lighthouse; Mrs Dalloway	Virginia Woolf
The Sorrows of Young Werther	Johann W. Goethe
Leaves of Grass - 1855 edition	Walt Whitman
Analects	Confucius
Beowulf	Anonymous
Plain Tales From The Hills	Rudyard Kipling
The Subjection of Women	John Stuart Mill
The Rights of Man	Thomas Paine
Progress and Poverty	Henry George
Captain Blood	Rafael Sabatini
Captains Courageous	Rudyard Kipling
The Meditations of Marcus Aurelius	Marcus Aurelius
The Social Contract	Jean Jacques Rousseau
War is a Racket	Smedley D. Butler
The Dead	James Joyce
The Old Wives' Tale	Arnold Bennett
Letters Concerning the English Nation	Voltaire
Portrait of the Artist As a Young Man	James Joyce
Coningsby	Benjamin Disraeli

Obtainable at all good online and local bookstores.
View Aziloth Books' full list at: www.azilothbooks.com

AZILOTH BOOKS — CHILDREN'S Classics

Aziloth Books is passionate about bringing the very best in children's classics fiction to the next generation of book-lovers. We believe in the transforming power of children's books to encourage a life-long love of reading, and publish only the best authors and illustrators. With its original design and outstanding quality, our highly successful list has something to suit every age and interest. Titles include:

The Railway Children	Edith Nesbit
Anne of Green Gables	Lucy Maud Montgomery
What Katy Did	Susan Coolidge
Puck of Pook's Hill	Rudyard Kipling
The Jungle Books	Rudyard Kipling
Just So Stories	Rudyard Kipling
Alice Through the Looking Glass	Charles Dodgson
*Alice's Adventures in Wonderland**	Charles Dodgson
Black Beauty	Anna Sewell
The War of the Worlds	H. G Wells
The Time Machine	H. G .Wells
The Sleeper Awakes	H. G. Wells
The Invisible Man	H. G. Wells
The Lost World	Sir Arthur Conan Doyle
*Gulliver's Travels**	Jonathan Swift
Catriona (David Balfour)	Robert Louis Stevenson
The Water Babies	Charles Kingsley
The First Men in the Moon	Jules Verne
The Secret Garden	Frances Hodgson Burnett
A Little Princess	Frances Hodgson Burnett
*Peter Pan**	J. M. Barrie
*The Song of Hiawatha**	Henry W. Longfellow
Tales from Shakespeare	Charles and Mary Lamb
The Wonderful Wizard of Oz	L. Frank Baum
The Complete Grimm's Fairy Tales	Jacob & Wilhelm Grimm

*with colour illustrations

Obtainable at all good online and local bookstores.
View Aziloth Books' full list at: www.azilothbooks.com

www.ingramcontent.com/pod-product-compliance
Lightning Source LLC
Chambersburg PA
CBHW071310060426
42444CB00034B/1768